The
Murder
of a
Shopping
Bag
Lady

The Murder of a Shopping Bag Lady

Brian Kates

Harcourt Brace Jovanovich, Publishers
San Diego   New York   London

Copyright © 1985 by Brian Kates

Requests for permission to make copies of any
part of the work should be mailed to: Permissions,
Harcourt Brace Jovanovich, Publishers, Orlando, FL 32887.

Library of Congress Cataloging in Publication Data
Kates, Brian.
The murder of a shopping bag lady.
Kates, Brian.
The murder of a shopping bag lady.
1. Iannotta, Phyllis.   2. Homeless woman—New York—
Biography.   3. Murder—New York—Case studies.   I. Title.
HV4506.N6K38   1985   364.1'523'0924 [B]   85-5867
ISBN 0-15-163540-4

Designed by Lucy Albanese
Printed in the United States of America
First Edition
A   B   C   D   E

THIS IS FOR MARY AND ELIZABETH
AND, ESPECIALLY, FOR MY PARENTS

*The words of my book nothing, the drift
of it every thing*

—WALT WHITMAN

Contents

Acknowledgments

To those who helped make this book happen I offer my deep appreciation, especially to Ann Quintano, for breaking bread; to my agent, Lewis Chambers, for his diligence; to Candace Leigh, for her encouragement; to Charlie McDade, for his insight; and to my editor, Sara Stein, for tempering my anger, helping to give shape to my thoughts, and providing good counsel above and beyond the call of duty.

And special thanks to all those who shared their time, their experience and their insight. Those not mentioned in the book include: Bill Armstrong, "Bagelman," Ellen Baxter, Andre Buonaiuto, John Clark, "Choctaw Pete" Dyer, Helene Fishman, Inspector Ed Forker, Lou Ganim, Frances Guttilla, Bob Hayes, Kim Hopper, Marcia Kramer, the Ladies of 13th Street, Bob Loomis, Janice Parker, Estelle Pettus, Sgt. Pete Sweeney, Betsy Weiss, Santi Visalli, and dozens of men and women of the streets whose names I never learned or who asked that I not identify them but who cared enough to show me the ropes.

All the events and characters in this book are real. Only the name Monica Lanza has been changed for her protection.

Introduction

The homeless, like the poor, have been with us always. What is new—or at least new to this generation—is the scale of the problem, the way it has come to intrude on our streets and neighborhoods, to embarrass us and perhaps to frighten us.

In "bag people" like Phyllis Iannotta, whose poignant story you are about to read—in the lives of our neighbors who struggle each day to find food, shelter, and an ounce of compassion—we see an indication of something larger that is happening to our country.

That something, I believe, recalls the words of an English statesman who over a century ago looked at the far-flung power of his nation and recognized a contradiction.

England, he wrote, was becoming two nations—one rich, the other poor; one hopeful, the other resentful; one confident, the other despairing.

So, too, the America of Phyllis Iannotta. We have become a *Tale of Two Cities*.

Although we recently experienced the worst economic crisis since the Great Depression, we still have managed in recent years to spend enormous sums in the pursuit of happiness, comfort, and recreation: $2 billion on video games, $10 billion on cosmetics, $25 billion on tobacco products, $56 billion on alcohol.

We also have embarked on the largest military buildup in our history, an expansion of our national arsenal that will require some $1.3 *trillion*.

At the same time, Washington has slashed relentlessly at programs that aid the poor, ultimately cutting food stamps by $6 billion, Medicaid by $4 billion, Aid to Families with Dependent Children by $2 billion, low-income housing by $19 billion.

The victims of these cuts are the citizens of the other America—the abject poor, the mentally disabled, those addicted to drugs or alcohol, the victims of racial and economic discrimination, of domestic violence, of broken homes and broken dreams, the homeless.

It is this second America—this nation of citizens without homes, this land of rag-wrapped nomads and rootless families—that Brian Kates has laid bare here.

It is an America that has spilled beyond the narrow confines of Skid Row to form a broad belt of decay across our nation. Its inhabitants include not just those who have always lived on the margins of American society, but also the so-called new poor—the men and women of the working class and middle class, blue-collar and white-collar, who have watched the collapse of the businesses and industries that put within their reach the American Dream: a steady job, a house, a pension, a hope of something better for their children.

It was that same dream that brought the infant Phyllis Iannotta to this country with her mother more than seventy years ago. They arrived here from Italy as my own family did, on a ship bound for Ellis Island, for a New World and a new life.

Phyllis Iannotta did not expect her piece of the American pie to be served on a silver platter. She knew she would have to work for it, and she did—quitting school during the Great Depression to support her impoverished family, working her way up from the dockside slums of Red Hook to the relative stability of Bay Ridge, Brooklyn.

A mental breakdown—apparently triggered when the man she loved walked out on her—sent her life into a tailspin. When she lost her sanity, she lost her home and, ultimately, her life, as she fell headlong through the massive holes in our "social safety net."

Since her death, homelessness has been the subject of two congressional hearings. The media have inundated us with stories about people living on our streets, under bridges, in drainage pipes, in makeshift shanties of cardboard and tin, in bus stations and old cars. And, of course, there have been the inevitable studies by governments, universities, and social agencies. They bring to mind Will Rogers's reaction when he learned the Roosevelt Administration had undertaken a series of studies on the plight of the farmer: "The commissions are just gathering data," he drawled. "They won't take the farmer's word for it that he is poor. They hire men to find out how poor he is. If they took all the money they spend on finding out how he is, and gave it to the farmer, he wouldn't need any more relief."

Despite the studies, despite the congressional hearings, despite the seemingly endless media stories, and despite the expenditure of millions upon millions of dollars for temporary shelter—$60 million a year in New York City alone—the ranks of the homeless in America have swelled to as many as 2.5 million men, women, and, saddest of all, children.

The reasons are startlingly clear. There is still a drastic shortage of housing for the poor, still no comprehensive plan for dealing with the mentally ill, still no national commitment to helping repair and redevelop the economies of those regions that face permanent decline.

I believe that the solution to the plight of the homeless, and to so many other of the problems that beset us and diminish us, begins in an idea taught by the generations of immigrants who made our history. It is the idea of family, of mutuality, of the sharing of benefits and burdens for the good of all. It requires the recognition that we can afford to be neither two nations nor a loose confederation of many selfish interest groups in which some classes or some individuals are judged less valuable than others, unworthy of help and expendable.

The idea of family isn't just a pretty notion or a pleasant abstraction. It is a principle of sound government, one that could have worked to save Phyllis Iannotta's life, one that can work now for America's homeless. But first we must admit that the homeless cannot be the concern solely of private charities or of one level of government but can be served only by a partnership that joins all our resources.

We must commit ourselves to the construction of new permanent and affordable housing in a program similar to Section 8, which subsidizes the rents of those who can no longer meet the prices of the housing market. We must agree to find ways to create supportive residences for the mentally handicapped in our communities. And we must be determined to repair and redevelop the deteriorated regions of our country racked by poverty, unemployment, and economic decay.

A generation ago John Steinbeck witnessed the pain and pathos of Americans thrust from their homes and dispossessed by the forces of a troubled economy. He described their agony as "a hunger in a stomach, multiplied a million times; a hunger in a single soul, multiplied a million times; muscles and minds aching to grow, to work, to create, multiplied a million times."

That ache and that hunger have not gone away, and in these pages Brian Kates provides a sobering look at the vineyards where today's grapes of wrath are sown. It is a frightening view in a mirror held up to us by the citizens of the other America.

"I guess the most horrible thing to me," a homeless woman told Kates one winter, "was the brutality of the ordinary citizen. By the end of the week, my feet were so covered with sores I could barely walk. I crawled uptown hugging the walls for support. And not a single human being offered me a helping hand."

Now is the time to extend that helping hand.

Governor Mario M. Cuomo
Albany, New York
July 1985

A Murder

Phyllis Iannotta died in the blended echo of her own screams and the crunch of her killer's shoes on broken glass. Her body was discarded amid a litter of wine bottles, used condoms, and human feces in a desolate parking lot in an enclave of Manhattan known as Hell's Kitchen.

She had been beaten, stabbed repeatedly, and raped. It was the savage conclusion to years of anguish and fear lived out in back alleys and doorways, of meals stolen from trash cans, of park benches called home.

Phyllis Iannotta was a shopping bag lady, one of the more than 6,000 women who make their homes on the streets of New York City. It was April 23, 1981. She was sixty-seven.

Her body was still there when I arrived, nearly three hours after a construction worker had discovered it lying

1

in a bloody heap next to a trash dumpster in a corner of the lot. It was so battered that at first he had not recognized its humanity.

The woman, older than my mother, was lying on her right side with a hideous grimace stretched across her face. She was wearing a black fake-fur coat and men's galoshes. There were deep cuts on her neck. Her maroon slacks had been yanked down below her ankles and her legs were caked with streaks of blood turned brown. To the right of the body, covered with pasty clots of blood, was the upper plate of her false teeth.

My hand trembled as I recorded the details in one of the long, narrow notebooks reporters carry everywhere.

Word of the killing had clacked into the *Daily News* city room at 9:30 that morning over the ancient black teletype machine that links the country's most widely read newspaper to the world's largest municipal police force:

PRESS 3 0930 HRS. 4-24-81 10 PCT

REPORT OF FEMALE FOUND DOA IN PARKING
LOT 40TH AND DYER AVE. APPROX 0735 HRS
THIS DATE. MULTIPLE STAB WOUNDS. VICTIM
BELIEVED HOMELESS. NO ARRESTS.

It was the third of nine messages that would be spewed out over the machine that day in a terse chronicle of murder and mayhem in the city's five boroughs.

It described what New York reporters call a "cheap homicide"—the killing of someone with few ties to the community in a neighborhood where killing is common: the slaying of a junkie in Harlem, say, or the stabbing of a man by his common-law wife during a drunken brawl in Bedford-Stuyvesant. In a city where nearly 2,000 murders are committed each year, editors do not attach much news value to such commonplace deaths.

At the tabloid *Daily News*, a "cheap homicide" is boiled down to two paragraphs and buried on an obscure page, if it's reported at all. Unless, that is, it has some special quality—something bizarre, ironic, or heart-touching—that lifts it above the mundane.

Metropolitan editor Dick Blood handed me the teletype message. "I want you to find out everything there is to know about this old lady," he ordered. "If she has a rich son living in some cushy Connecticut suburb, I want to know about it. If her bags were stuffed with dollar bills, I want the serial numbers. Got it? No stone unturned . . ."

Blood, who prides himself on being an old-style editor—three-quarters martinet, one-quarter mentor—had decided this murder might have that special, elusive quality that would make it news. It was my job to find out.

The seven-block walk along 42nd Street took only fifteen minutes, but it carried me across cultures from fashionable Murray Hill on the East Side to the dockside squalor of Hell's Kitchen on the West.

Forty-second Street is Manhattan's main crosstown artery. It defines midtown and feeds Times Square. It is the fast lane of the city's tenderloin. Here, a kaleidoscope of bright lights mixes with a cacophony of voices hawking sex and drugs night and day, every day.

At Fifth Avenue, I crossed to the West Side and climbed the granite steps leading past the neoclassic solidity of the

3

New York Public Library and cut across Bryant Park, trailed by a dozen teenagers proffering everything from pot to heroin. "Loose joints, rrreeeefer, man, good smoke . . . Upsdownsupsdownsupsdownsupsdowns . . . Get 'em. Ups. Downs. Elevator man's here. Black beauties. Ludes. Dust. Good coke."

Beyond the park, from Sixth Avenue to the whore-stroll on Eighth Avenue known as the "Minnesota Strip," I counted seventeen porno bookstores, five live-show peep parlors, twenty X-rated-movie houses, six head shops, and four stores with plate-glass windows stuffed with chukka sticks, handcuffs, come-along grips, machetes, and gravity-blade knives.

On Eighth Avenue the bars were full. Pimps in wide-brimmed hats and $200 shoes sipped tall drinks while their girls hustled Jersey boys from across the river—the bridge-and-tunnel trade, they call it—at $15 a pop. "You goin' out hon? Show you a real good time."

Outside the Avon Theater, teenage boys in tight jeans loitered suggestively, flashing sly looks that promised quick, anonymous sex. The sign on the marquee proclaimed: "Body Love—All Seats $1.99." Through the glass door another sign was visible: "Beware of Pickpockets."

Monte players with $20 bills laced between their fingers rapped their hypnotic jive as they flipped the three bent cards onto upturned cardboard boxes:

> *"Pick the red, forget the black.*
> *Goin' home to pick up the slack.*
> *Pick the red, get yo' money back."*

I crossed Ninth Avenue and walked south to 40th Street. Boarded windows of derelict buildings and piles of uncol-

4

lected garbage signaled the entrance to Hell's Kitchen. Here, the bright lights gave way to a collection of drab warehouses and tenements, and the people, frayed by the constant threat of violence and ground into listlessness by poverty, stared back at me with vacant eyes.

But even they could be counted on to congregate in the aftermath of violence. Down the street a small crowd had assembled at the entrance to a parking lot, like a giant X marking the spot where something terrible had happened.

The lot, which occupies more than half a city block, was where the Port Authority of New York and New Jersey parked the fleet of buses that shuttle commuters through the Lincoln Tunnel under the Hudson River less than a block away. Workmen at a construction project in the Port Authority Bus Terminal across the street also parked their cars there. But that day two police vehicles blocked the entrance, barring the crowd from the activity inside. Uniformed cops and detectives swarmed over the scene.

The onlookers heatedly traded theories. Some already had the murder half solved. But, as in all crowds, the consensus was loudly divided. Half argued that the killer had to be one of the junkies from Daytop Village, the addict-rehabilitation center across the street; the other half was ready to pin the rap on one of the feral youths of Covenant House, a residence for runaway teenagers two blocks away.

If Donald Longo, detective second grade, tenth precinct, NYPD, had any theories, he was keeping them to himself. Burly and balding, he stood, dressed in a gray three-piece suit, in the center of a cluster of cops. There was little doubt that he was in charge.

Flashing the press pass that entitles reporters to "pass police and fire lines wherever formed," I walked past the uniformed officers at the entrance to the lot and approached him. "Excuse me," I said, after waiting for him to finish briefing the officers. "I'm with the *Daily News*. Can you tell me what happened here?"

"Not now," he said. It was more a command than a statement.

"I'm right on deadline," I lied. "Can you tell me anything at all? Just the basics."

The detective sighed. "Look," he said. "An elderly woman has been killed. Beaten very badly. Multiple stab wounds. Possibly sexually assaulted. Okay?"

"Do you have an ID yet?"

He nodded. "Phyllis Iannotta, female/white, age sixty-seven. She lived around the corner in the shelter." He gestured to a five-story tenement at the edge of the parking lot. "The nuns took her in. They call it the Dwelling Place. It's a shelter. You know, for shopping bag ladies. She was staying there. Now you know as much as I do." He was smiling, but the words came out flat and cold.

I pressed. "You find the weapon?"

Longo shook his head.

"Do you have a motive?"

"No," he answered. He turned and walked briskly from the lot. "Come to the precinct later and I'll tell you whatever I can," he called over his shoulder. "Right now I got other things to do. Okay?" He was busy coordinating the massive effort that attends even a "cheap homicide."

Ten yards away, at the rear of the old Lamston's five-and-ten, next to a large, green trash dumpster, the body of Phyllis Iannotta lay under a brown blanket that a policeman had found under the spare tire in the trunk of his squad car. It was torn and spotted with grease. Nearly two

6

hours before, a priest had offered the last rites of the Roman Catholic Church over the lifeless form under the blanket, and an assistant medical examiner had been summoned to reduce the savage beating, the tearing of flesh and the breaking of bone, to a few lines on a yellow Department of Health death certificate:

"Contusions, abrasions and lacerations of hand, face, body and extremities. Stab wounds (3) of neck and pelvis. Fractures of skull, ribs, and finger. Intermeningeal hemorrhage. HOMICIDE."

Forensic experts had already combed the lot for scraps of evidence, taken measurements, made diagrams, and departed. Uniformed cops had recorded the license-plate numbers of every car in the lot so their owners could be questioned. Detectives had fanned out in the neighborhood, knocking on doors and asking questions: Where were you last night? What did you see? Did you hear anything?

As I approached the body, a police photographer pulled away the blanket and systematically began snapping pictures. I took one look at the corpse and felt a spasm jerk in my stomach and burn its way to my throat. I hurried to get out of the lot.

Most of the onlookers had dispersed. They had begun to drift away when the cops started asking questions. Only one spectator remained, a gray-haired woman in her sixties. She was standing across the street in front of the church, a solitary figure in bedroom slippers and a tired blue house dress. She gazed intently toward the lot. A smoking cigarette hung from her lips.

I joined her at the curb. "A terrible thing," I offered.

She nodded.

"You live around here?"

She nodded again. "In there," she said, gesturing toward the narrow four-story walkup behind us.

I introduced myself.

"Helen," she said. "Helen Kehayas." Her eyes never left the parking lot.

"The dead woman," I said, pulling out my notebook. "She lived in the shelter across the street. The Dwelling Place. The police say her name was Iannotta. Phyllis Iannotta. Did you know her, maybe see her around the neighborhood?"

"I dunno," she began. "You see all these women, sad women, going in and out. Got nothing but the stuff in their bags. Old clothes and all. I say hello. Sometimes they say hello back. Like that. Not like you'd call them a friend or anything. But they're people like anybody else. Sometimes I think I could have been like one of them, you know, no place to go."

She paused and looked at me. "See, when I got burned out of my old place four years ago, it took me months to find this place. Me and my daughter Lisa, she's a language tutor, we wound up staying in cheap hotels, real fleabags some of them. We borrowed money. That's what we lived on. See, I'm disabled. Can't work. Used to sing in cabarets. Greek places. Oh, them was the days. But no more. Anyway, it was lucky for me I had some friends. But you can't sponge off your friends and your family forever. If I hadn't found this place, you can bet in a couple more months you'da found me on the streets too."

She took a drag on her cigarette, exhaled loudly, and flicked the butt into the gutter. "Now I look at them ladies and I say to myself, 'There but for the grace of God . . .'"

"What about last night?" I asked her. "Did you see or hear anything unusual?"

8

"Cops asked me the same thing," she said.

"What did you tell them?"

Kehayas pulled another cigarette from her pack, lit it, and inhaled deeply. "You like a cup of coffee?" she asked.

The apartment, neat and spotlessly clean with a brown shag rug and early-American furniture, seemed out of place amid the chaos of Hell's Kitchen. On the walls were photos of Kehayas's pretty dark-haired daughter at her first communion, her graduation from high school, receiving her college diploma. House plants flourished on a windowsill. A twenty-seven-inch Zenith color television dominated one corner of the small room.

Kehayas emerged from the kitchen with a steaming cup of coffee, handed it to me, and settled into an easy chair. She lit a cigarette with the embers from another. "It was about one in the morning," she began. "I know because 'MacMillan and Wife' was on. I was watching it while I waited for Lisa to come home. See, she moonlights as a cocktail hostess so we can make ends meet. Well, anyhow, she should have been home long ago, so I'm worried. You know, this ain't no place for a girl to be out late at night."

Kehayas described her fears of the prostitutes who gathered every night on the corner up the street. Many of them, she knew, were transvestites—"he-shes," cops call them—with prison records and a reputation for violence. She had heard and believed the rumor that a few years before one of them had robbed a john and cut off his penis with a straight razor.

"They disgust me and I'm afraid of some of them," she said with a shudder. "And then there's the goddamn junkies shooting up in the doorways. You walk past and there they are shooting up right in front of your eyes. They don't give a damn about anything. They could jump out and rob you, just like that. They do it all the time. Then there are the kids. They go around terrorizing people, beating up on women, taking their money. I'm telling you this is a bad place to live. But what choice do we have? I learned my lesson four years ago. If you've got a place, you hang onto it. Believe me."

"About last night," I said. "What happened?"

"Well, like I said, I was waiting for Lisa and I was worried, as any mother would be, and I was trying to keep my mind off it with TV. During the commercials, I'd go into the kitchen and wash some dishes. Well, I was in there with the water running when I hear this scream. This horrible scream. I couldn't move for half a minute it scared me so much. Then the first thing I thought of was Lisa. It just shot through my mind. So I ran over to the window and I looked out."

Rain was beating against the glass. "All I could see was this old woman on the stoop across the street," Kehayas said. "She had on a dark coat and she had a big shopping bag full of stuff. I figured it was one of them bag ladies the nuns took in. You see them all hours of the night in all kinds of weather. Didn't see nothing unusual in that, you know. I thought maybe I seen her before. But I dunno.

"Anyhow, there was this colored fella and he come up to her and stood so I couldn't see her. He was a young fella, nothing special about him that you'd remember. He was wearing a blue and white jacket and sneakers. That's all I could tell you about him. I dunno. It was raining and that made it hard to see, but it looked to me like he was just talking to her. So I didn't think nothin' of it."

Moments later, the sound of her daughter putting the key in the lock had brought a sweeping sense of relief. "I gave her a piece of my mind, anyway," Kehayas told me. "I said, 'Lisa, that could have been you.' I told her, 'I was so worried I was going to call the police.' But she just laughed at me. 'Call the police?' she said. 'For a scream? In this neighborhood?' She was right. You hear screams all the time around here."

Still, Kehayas could not block out the memory of the scream. As she talked to her daughter she pushed the curtain back from the window and looked again into the night. The old woman was gone. The man was gone. All she saw was the rain.

"I don't think it would have made any difference if I had called the police," she said. "Maybe it was somebody else who screamed, right? I mean, who knows?" She chain-lit another cigarette and brushed the fallen ashes from her dress into the palm of her hand and deposited them into an ashtray. She avoided my eyes. "Anyway, I've called the police before and they never come."

It was after noon when I left Helen Kahayas. Detective Longo and most of the other cops had filtered from the lot, but the body of Phyllis Iannotta still lay under the brown blanket on the asphalt awaiting its trip to the morgue in the medical examiner's Black Maria.

Two cops sat in a squad car guarding the entrance to the lot under a sign that warned: "No Trespassing. Violators will be Prosecuted." Local kids had covered the sign with their marks, mocking its admonition in red spray paint: Freddy, Zooty, Space Case, Near II, Mr. Kool, Murf.

I leaned against the blue and white car and showed them my press pass. "You guys know who found the body?" I asked. They looked at each other. "I dunno," one of them said. "Somebody said it was a construction guy. Found her when he came to work." He chuckled. "Great way to start the day, huh?"

"You got the guy's name?"

"Beats me," the cop said. But I noticed on the clipboard next to him were written the words Dom Nisi, construction worker, in large letters.

Ten minutes later I was sitting in a makeshift office in the old Lamston's five-and-ten, which had been converted into a headquarters for the construction project at the Port Authority Bus Terminal across the street. Dominick Nisi, the construction foreman, rose from his seat in front of a sawhorse table covered with blueprints. I introduced myself. He extended his hand. He was in his early fifties, short, but trim, with a firm grip.

Nisi told me that he had arrived at work from his home in suburban Scarsdale about seven o'clock, as he did every morning. He parked his Volkswagen in the Port Authority lot and walked up 40th Street past the block-long line of shopping bag ladies who were waiting for breakfast at the Dwelling Place.

"I never get used to it," he said. "I see those old ladies and I think of my kid, you know, and I just sort of pray that nothing like that would ever happen to her."

That morning when Nisi arrived he found the lock at the entrance had been broken and the hinges had been tampered with. "That really teed me off," he said. "It's not the first time we've been broken into and it always costs us time and that means money and we've got to finish on budget. So I walked across the street to the police station in the bus terminal to get a cop."

Minutes later, Nisi returned with Port Authority police officer Charles Desfosse. Together they searched the building. Nothing seemed to be missing, so Desfosse returned to the terminal and Nisi sat down to work at the pile of plans sprawled on the plywood sawhorse table that served him as a desk. "The thing just kept nagging at me, you know. I figured somebody *had* to have broken in and it bugged me that nothing was missing. So I went to take a second look."

This time, he did find something. The burglar alarm over the entrance to the loading dock at the rear of the building had been ripped off the wall. Nisi bent down and pulled up the massive rolling-shutter door. Standing on the loading bay, he surveyed the lot where only half an hour before he had parked his car. Nothing seemed amiss and he started to pull the heavy door shut. Then he saw it.

"God," he said. "I didn't even realize what it was at first. Then it registered. What I was looking at, this thing, was a human body. A woman. She was nude from the waist down. She was mutilated. Her head was bashed in."

Nisi spoke calmly but his hands trembled slightly as he spoke. "You'll have to forgive me," he said. "I'm still a little shook up." It was the first time, he told me, that he had ever seen a dead human being anywhere but in a funeral home. "What I did," he continued, "was sort of look at her stomach for some sign of breathing. But there wasn't any. She was just lying there. There was blood everywhere . . ."

Nisi said he ran back across the street to the police station. Desfosse was preparing to take his post directing bus traffic on the second level of the cavernous terminal. "You know, that guy said he'd been a cop for more than twenty years and he'd never seen anything like that. I'm telling you, it was beyond describing. Horrible. Inhuman."

13

Later, Desfosse, a veteran who boasted that he'd "arrested people for every crime there is except treason," told me, "I thought I was going to toss my cookies it was so bloody, so savage. The body was covered with gore. I tell you, you see that and you wonder, 'Who in God's name could have done something like that?' Then you realize that part of your job as a cop is to find out. I got on the radio and told the desk sergeant to notify the detectives and the medical examiner's office. Then I went over to the shelter to see if one of the nuns could ID the body."

The words Dwelling Place appeared in Old English script on the battered red door at 409 West 40th Street. I rang the doorbell and waited, expecting a black-habited nun to materialize and usher me inside. Instead, a chunky woman wearing a blue-plaid flannel shirt and workman's overalls came to the door. She had short, dark, curly hair and I put her somewhere in her early thirties. "You must be here about Phyllis," she said. I nodded and identified myself.

"I'm Sister Nancy," she said. She forced a smile. "We're really not ready to see anybody. I hope you can understand."

"I'll only take a few minutes of your time," I tried.

"I'm sorry. Maybe later. Come back later," she suggested, and she closed the door gently in my face.

As I walked up the street, I passed an old woman huddled in the doorway of the adjacent building. She was wearing an old pair of men's black oxford shoes and a heavy winter coat unbuttoned to reveal only a tattered slip. I approached her cautiously. "Did you know the woman who was murdered?"

"You with the television?" she asked in a voice that could

shatter glass. I shook my head. "No," I told her, "the *Daily News*. I'm here about the woman who was murdered. Did you know her?"

"Phyllis," she said. "I didn't know her real good. But she was nice. She didn't never hurt nobody. Why did they do that to her?"

"I don't know," I told her.

"Do they know who done it?"

I shrugged.

"Will they catch the guy?"

"I don't know," I said.

"Well I hope they catch him fast. It makes me afraid to know he's out here somewhere. I hope the cops are doing something. They're never around when you need them."

I jogged the mile to the tenth precinct, arriving as a detective was dragging an elderly woman up the granite steps of the station house. She was slightly built and her right hand was swathed in gauze bandage. She was yelling: "They're kidnapping me, goddamn it. Somebody help me! They're kidnapping me!"

The detective hustled her by the arm through the massive green doors, past the desk, and up to the second-floor squad room. The desk sergeant, a burly veteran with silver hair and a flamboyant handlebar mustache, watched with amused detachment. "Gonna sell her into the white slave trade," he deadpanned. He turned toward me. "And what can I do for you?"

I told him. He shrugged, picked up the phone, and dialed the detectives upstairs. "Guy down here from the *News* wants to talk to Detective Longo about the bag lady murder," he said. He hung up. "Gonna be a while," he said.

15

"You can wait if you want. They're kinda busy up there."

After ten minutes of pacing the marble floor and reading wanted posters I grew restless. I told the desk sergeant I'd be back in a few minutes, left the station, and found a phone on the corner. I called Dick Blood.

"So?" he began. "What've you got?"

"It's pretty grisly," I told him. "Victim was beaten, stabbed, maybe raped. Not very pretty. No photo possibility, that's for sure. I got the basics: woman's name, age, all that stuff. She lived in a shelter for homeless women adjacent to the parking lot. It's run by some nuns. I tried to talk to them, but they were pretty broken up. Told me to come back later.

"Talked to an old lady who lives across the street. Thinks she heard somebody screaming around one-thirty in the morning. Looks out the window sees a black guy in sneakers talking to a bag lady on the stoop. Probably the victim. Anyhow, cops say they have no motive. No weapon recovered. Random thing, I guess. I'll know more after I talk to the detective."

Blood waited until I'd finished. "As a murder, it's pretty cheap. Not much of a story," he said. "But it's got human interest. Might turn into something good. You've got a couple of hours before deadline. Let's wait until we get some more detail. Stuff on the dead woman, where she came from, how she wound up at the shelter, all that. See what you can find out from the cops, then get your ass back to that shelter."

When I returned to the station house, the desk sergeant told me Longo could see me now. I climbed the narrow stairs and entered the squad room. It was like every squad room I'd ever been in at the older police stations: walls two-tone institutional green, more desks than there was room for, all bunched together to save space, mismatched furniture, duty charts on the wall. Everything old and dusty. Shabby.

Longo was sitting on the edge of a battered desk the color of gunmetal. With him was the detective who had hauled in the old lady when I arrived.

"Thanks for seeing me," I said. "I know you're real busy."

Longo nodded, then turned to his partner. "This gentleman is with the *Daily News*," he said. "So watch what you say, okay?"

I smiled. "I hear you sold that old lady into slavery."

Longo laughed. "Yeah," he said. "Mitkish here is a notorious slaver. Right, John?"

"Cute," the detective said. "Real cute." A six-foot Clint Walker look-alike with the exaggerated deltoids of a bodybuilder, Mitkish walked to the end of the squad room. "I think I'll go get started on my paperwork," he said, leaving Longo to deal with me.

"So," I asked, "how are you making out?"

"The truth? Not real well. Got no weapon. No motive. No real witnesses. You know, you ask a question and they say, 'What me? I didn't see nothin'.' The usual routine. You know that old woman John brought in? She was my one big hope. We learned she was with the Iannotta woman last night. You saw that big bandage on her hand?" I nodded.

"Looks like the guy who killed the Iannotta woman also attacked her. Apparently they were sitting on the stoop next door when this guy struck. He hit this gal, the witness I mean, with a crowbar or a pipe or something. She put up her hands in self-defense, got her finger broken. After that she ran. We had to hunt her down. Sure as hell she knows

17

what happened to Iannotta. But we can't get anything out of her. Nothing. I mean, she's scared."

"What's her name?" I asked.

Longo smiled and shook his head. "You know better than to ask me that. She's a witness. I can't let you have her name. No way."

"How'd you find her?"

Longo looked around the squad room. He called out, "Mitkish! C'mere. Tell the *Daily News* reporter how you found our witness. And, John, no names please."

Mitkish poured himself a cup of coffee. He delved into a pocket and dropped a quarter in the kitty next to the pot. He walked slowly over to Longo's desk.

"We had a description of this woman who was supposed to be like the key witness in this thing," he began. "It was not such a hot description except for the bandage, which is a pretty strong detail, right? So, anyway, I'm canvassing the neighborhood, asking questions, doing my thing, when I happen to look across the street and there's this bag lady with a bandage on her hand. Got to be her, right? So I run across the street, tell her I'm a police officer, and tell her I want to ask her a few questions. She tried to run, but I grabbed her.

"So I'm getting her across the street when this car comes racing up, screeches the brakes and these guys jump out with guns and one of them shouts, like he's in the movies: 'Police!' I take one look at these guys—they're Port Authority types, right?—and I say, '*I'm* a cop, goddamn it!' " The three of us laughed. "So after all that," Mitkish concluded, "the old lady decides she don't wanna talk." He shook his head. "People ask me why I want to be a cop. Times like this, I don't know myself."

Mitkish said he took the woman back to the parking lot to "refresh her memory." But, he said, "She became hysterical and after that the more we questioned her the more frantic and irrational she became."

"If Iannotta was on the stoop on 40th Street," I asked Longo, "how did she wind up back in the lot? He drag her there or what?"

"Dunno," Longo said. "Maybe. Maybe he lured her back there. That's one of the big questions. There was some blood on the stoop, but we don't know whether it was Iannotta's or the witness's. Maybe we'll never know."

I checked my watch. It was nearly 2:30. "So," I asked, "where can I find this lady, your witness?"

Mitkish glanced at Longo, who nodded. "Took her back to the shelter," Mitkish said.

"Thanks," I said. "I'll keep in touch."

"By the way," Longo said as I was leaving. "As long as you're going back there, I don't know if you noticed before. Iannotta's shopping bag was busted open and the contents were scattered out on the sidewalk in front of the stoop. We know it was hers because the nuns said she left with a bag and the other woman didn't. Nothing in it of any investigative value. But you might be able to use it. You know. What do you guys call it?"

"Color?"

"Right. Color."

I made a note of it.

Two doors down from the Dwelling Place, in front of the stoop that Helen Kehayas had watched through the driving rain, the contents of Phyllis Iannotta's shopping bag were strewn across the sidewalk: a bag of Martinson's coffee, a vial of Tempo perfume, a ball of dirty white yarn, two shabby cardigan sweaters, an empty box of Sloan's liniment, a can of Friskies turkey-and-giblets cat food, and a plastic spoon.

The same chunky young nun answered the Dwelling Place door. "You came back," she said. She sounded surprised. "I'm glad. I didn't mean to be rude. It's just that we've all been through a lot today." She opened the door and stepped back. "Please," she said, "come in. Most of the ladies are out of the house now. They go out during the day. It will be quiet and we can talk."

I followed her up a long, narrow flight of stairs, past a hand-lettered sign that read: "Dwelling Place. Peace to All Who Enter." She led me into a large living room on the second floor. Shreds of crepe paper and a few half-deflated balloons hung from the ceiling, the vestiges, she explained, of an Easter party five days before. She motioned me into an armchair by a window overlooking 40th Street and settled herself into the chair beside it. The room smelled of Pinesol.

"Phyllis first came here for meals in the winter of '79," Sister Nancy began. "Before that, she was living in the streets, sleeping in doorways or in the Port Authority Bus Terminal. She should probably have been in a hospital. She had hallucinations, heard voices. She was a very pleasant person most of the time. I really loved her. But she was also very angry. Sometimes she'd fly off the handle, yell and scream. She had a real mouth on her. She wasn't so different from a lot of the ladies in that respect. We see the results of their anger, but we rarely get to understand where exactly it comes from."

"So," I asked, "why wasn't she in a hospital?"

The nun laughed without a trace of humor. "Well, she wasn't about to commit herself to a hospital," she said. "And the state wouldn't commit her unless she was homicidal or suicidal. That's the law. Phyllis wasn't holding a gun to anybody's head, so she couldn't get the help she needed. Simple as that. That's a fact of life around here."

"What are the other facts of existence here?" I asked.

Sister Nancy shook her head. "Rotation," she said. "That's *the* fact of our existence."

She saw my puzzled look. "You see," she explained, "we only have beds here for twelve women and we let twelve more women sleep sitting up in chairs. But there are thousands of women out there"—she gestured toward the streets outside—"thousands who have no place to live. So many ladies come here for shelter that we can only let them stay for four days before we send them back out on the streets. We call it 'rotation.' Four days in, three days out. It's horrible, but we don't have much choice."

I sensed what was coming. "And Phyllis?" I asked.

Sister Nancy shook her head slowly as if to erase what she was about to say. "Yes," she said wearily. "Phyllis was on rotation."

Phyllis and her friend Monica Lanza had left the Dwelling Place on rotation after dinner that night. "It was about eight, eight-thirty I guess," Sister Nancy said. "Then, I guess it was around one in the morning, Monica came back. She was pounding on the door and screaming her head off. I was in bed and Jonah, she works the overnight shift, ran downstairs to see what all the fuss was about.

"It was Monica, and she had a cut on her head and on her hand. She said some guy hit her with a pipe or something. Jonah tried to find out what happened, but Monica

21

was very agitated. She wasn't making a whole lot of sense, as you can imagine, and she wouldn't let anybody treat the wounds. So Jonah figured the best thing to do was give her some tea, calm her down, and put her to bed. Jonah asked her about Phyllis, but she said she didn't know where she went. Phyllis was a loner; just because she and Monica left together was no reason to assume that they'd stayed together." She shook her head. "Now, the police seem to think whoever attacked Monica killed Phyllis."

I looked up from my notes into the nun's eyes. They were fixed on a hand-lettered sign on the far wall: "Be Hidden, Be a Light. Go Without Fear into the Depths of Men's Hearts."

The irony was not lost on her. "Phyllis hated rotation. She was afraid. Just a month ago, she came back all bloodied up because somebody beat her up. She had a cut on her head, a bloody nose, and a split lip. Said some man had offered her money to go with him and when she refused he beat her up." She paused, thinking. "It's not so uncommon, you know. These ladies make easy targets. They are very vulnerable, and whenever somebody is weak, there will always be someone ready to take advantage of it."

I checked my watch. I'd been at the Dwelling Place nearly an hour. If I was going to make the edition, I had to get back to the city room and start writing. "One more question," I said, pulling myself out of the chair. "What did Phyllis look like? Was she short or tall, slim or heavy or what? It would help for me to get a mental picture of her."

Sister Nancy smiled for the first time since we began talking. "She was quite short. Not five feet, I'll bet, and a little bent over. She had salt-and-pepper hair and glasses, thick glasses . . ." She stopped. "Wait here a minute." She practically jumped out of her chair. "I'll be right back."

The young nun returned a few minutes later with a three-by-three Polaroid snapshot, which she placed gently in my hand. It showed a cluster of women eating at a large table covered with brightly colored oilcloth and laden with dishes of food.

"It's from last Thanksgiving," the nun said. "That one's Phyllis." She pointed to a woman in the far right corner of the picture.

The woman had gray hair cropped short. A pair of dark-rimmed glasses were propped on a large, sharp nose. She wore a heavy brown cardigan over a blue print blouse. Between the fingers of her left hand she held a lighted cigarette, and on her face she wore a smile—a grin, really, filled with puckish good humor.

"She was a little elf," Sister Nancy said.

I left the Dwelling Place with a full notebook. I had my story: the brutal and senseless murder, the horror of the nightly rotations, the pathetic inventory of the scattered shopping bag. It was all there. I was pleased with myself, and as I walked back to the Daily News Building along 42nd Street, I began to compose a lead.

But my mind strayed beyond the 600-word story that could be written in thirty minutes from information gathered in a few hours. That was the story of what Phyllis Iannotta had become, not of who she had been. The real story went beyond the battered corpse, now in the morgue, beyond the old woman with her shopping bags sleeping in doorways. The real story was Phyllis herself. Who had she been? How had she wound up on the streets? No little girl grows to womanhood with the dream of becoming a shopping bag lady. Who *was* Phyllis Iannotta?

Just
a Story

The account of Phyllis Iannotta's murder fought for attention on page five of the *Daily News* the next day, a day
when readers also would learn that President Reagan had
lifted the Soviet grain embargo; that Atlanta police had no
new clues in their search for the killer of twenty-five black
youths; that a federal prosecutor had raked New Jersey
Senator Harrison Williams over the coals for the third straight
day in the ABSCAM congressional bribery trial.

The headline read:

DEATH OF A SHOPPING BAG LADY
VICTIMIZED BY LIFE, SHE ENDS UP KILLER'S VICTIM

It was just another story, better than some, not as good
as others. I had written hundreds of such stories over the

24

years until they had all begun to blend together. Who could remember them all? Unkept political promises, official corruption, children burned in fires, plane crashes, murders. Just change the names and dates; they're all the same. Bang them out—mechanically phrased epics of 600 words or less—and keep your eye out for the twist, the new angle, the irony that will make this story different from the one last week.

The making of a cynic begins early in a newspaperman's career. I got my first taste of what would become an almost daily diet of tragedy within a week after taking my first newspaper job as a $125-a-week reporter.

The paper had received a call that a man had just fallen off the city pier not far from the paper's editorial offices. The editor hiked his thumb in my direction. "Get down to the river and check it out," he ordered.

I ran the five blocks to the pier and got there just in time to see the man sink into the gray-brown Hudson for the last time. Several members of the local volunteer life-saving corps had launched a boat to rescue him, but they weren't able to reach him in time. I helped them pull the corpse to shore, then asked one of them what had happened. He shrugged. "Ask him," he said, pointing to a black boy, ten, maybe eleven years old, who stood about fifteen yards away surrounded by a clutter of fishing poles, bait buckets, and rusty crab traps. The boy's hands were thrust deep into the pockets of his jeans and he was watching us intently.

I approached the youngster, kneeled in front of him, and asked if he had seen what had happened. He nodded and told me that he had been fishing off the pier when the man approached him and asked if he could borrow one of his fishing poles. The boy said sure. But he told the man he didn't have any more hooks. So the man gave him a dollar and sent him up the street to buy some. "I kept the change, just like he said," the boy told me, jiggling two quarters in his palm.

The man had been drinking, and when he tried to open the plastic packet, the hooks spilled out into the water. "And you know what he did then?" the boy asked. I shook my head. "He jumped right in after 'em."

The youngster fell silent, and I realized that this little boy had just seen a man drown—had watched him go down once, then once again, coughing and sputtering and yelling for help before he finally sank for the last time. And he had watched us pull the corpse from the river, too, with snot and vomit spilling out of the nose and mouth. It was an ugly sight, and it occurred to me as I recorded the boy's words in my notebook that he had probably just seen death for the first time and that he might even feel somewhat responsible.

"Are you okay?" I asked. I tried to sound fatherly. "How about letting me take you home?"

The boy barely masked his disdain. "Are you kidding?" he said. "I cut school today, and I ain't finished fishin'."

With that, he collected his gear, walked back to the pier, and swung a crab trap out over the murky water. It splashed into the Hudson only a few feet from the spot where the man had drowned. I came back to the newsroom and told the story to my editor. When I got to the part about the kid, he clapped his hands in glee. "I love it. I love it. Oh yeah. Terrific. Oh yeah." He hadn't been interested much in the guy who drowned. But the boy—that was page-one stuff.

So it goes. Many such stories—"good stories," I'd come to call them—would follow over the years: the Christmas Eve fire that killed four young children, destroying their house but leaving virtually untouched a brand new bike leaning against a charred tree; the hour-old baby found in a garbage can wrapped in a garish pink nightgown; the holocaust in the old Blue Angel night club; the nightly horror of Son of Sam; the Murder at the Metropolitan Opera; Jean Harris and the killing of the Scarsdale Diet Doctor, and on and on. They became just stories—hastily written deadline dramas reduced to simple formulas to be digested easily by readers over their morning coffee. Small wonder journalists build up a crustacean cynicism. It helps us keep our perspective, our cherished objectivity. Which is another way of saying that we often trade our feelings for our sanity.

But with Phyllis Iannotta it was different. She was not just another story. I couldn't leave her as a journalistic cliché. She didn't fit the myth. Nothing I had seen that day upheld the illusion perpetuated in the semifiction of the tabloids that shopping-bag ladies are romantic vagabonds, passionately independent eccentrics, charming madwomen with fortunes squirreled away in their bags.

The jumble of relics spilled from Phyllis Iannotta's shopping bag testified to a different truth.

Two months before I had had a brief taste of what I imagined Phyllis Iannotta's life had been like. It had begun as a story—just a story—in a series of articles I wrote on homelessness in New York. I was to pose as a homeless man, to spend a day in the streets, to eat on the breadlines and sleep in a flophouse. Simple enough.

The Men's Shelter is a dirty red-brick building, four stories tall, on East 3rd Street just off the Bowery. Here men were "processed" and issued vouchers good for "three hots and a cot" in a Bowery flophouse.

I arrived there at 2:00 P.M. on a Thursday in the middle of February dressed in torn bell-bottom jeans, an old work shirt, a gray hooded sweatshirt, my old green Army over-coat, and a black watchman's cap. I took with me no iden-tification and only $3. I brought along a pack of Pall Malls, even though I hadn't smoked in years. Cigarettes are cur-rency on the streets. They sell for a dime apiece. Few bums can afford the price of a whole pack; they buy them one at a time.

I carried a tiny red spiral-bound notebook I had bought at Woolworth's for fifty-five cents. In it I would record my observations.

The tiled floor of the shelter was littered with Styrofoam cups and old newspapers. The stench was like a slap in the face: vomit, sweat, stale tobacco, and disinfectant. At least 200 men were milling around the room in tattered clothes and mismatched shoes; more still were collapsed in green molded-plastic chairs; some were passed out on the floor in the corners of the room.

Many of them were black with greasy filth from nights spent in gutters and on warm subway gratings; the faces of some bore blood-caked wounds from drunken falls or the beatings of jackrollers.

They searched with grimy hands through layers of cloth-ing for the itching bites of lice and bedbugs, fitfully reaching up their pants legs, clawing at their crotches, scratching their scalps until they bled.

Everything seemed to be happening in slow motion like the dreams in movies. I moved farther into the room. To the right there was a small room with a Dutch door where three uniformed guards sat playing cards. I called into the room, "Where do I go to get a meal and a place for the night?"

Without looking up from his hand, one of them said, "Go to Window 1." On a bulletin board behind him, along with various administrative notices and wanted posters, was a crudely drawn cartoon. It showed a man pissing into a fan. Under it were the words "Skel takes a shower."

I took my place on a line in front of Window 1 and waited. I did not know what I was waiting for. I was just doing what I was told. It reminded me of boot camp. Hurry up and wait. The line moved at a snail's pace. In fifteen minutes I'd advanced one step. The waiting seemed to make everyone edgy. You could sense the tension on the line like a physical presence.

An old derelict accidentally jostled the young man in front of him. The youth spun around and exploded. "Get the fuck out of here," he shouted. "Get your fuckin' ass out of here!" He was no more than twenty, tall and muscular with prison tattoos across his knuckles: L-O-V-E in crude blue letters on the right hand, H-A-T-E on the left. He shoved the old man once, then once again, and bullied him into a corner, where he slapped him again and again with short flicks of his hand.

Another man stepped between them. "Why don't you pick on *me*?" he challenged. The two were squaring off, posturing and pushing like boys before a schoolyard fight, when two burly guards moved in, banging cudgels the size of table legs. "Awright, skels, let's go. Into the Big Room. C'mon. Move it." They herded us out of the reception area. It seemed part of the Alice-in-Wonderland logic of the Men's Shelter that the "Big Room" was much smaller than the other.

There were only a few chairs, all of them linked together

so they couldn't be removed or picked up and thrown, and they were quickly taken with much pushing and shoving. The weakest remained standing. I put my back against a wall and watched.

A sneak thief slithered among the human wreckage. He had pulled the hood of his sweatshirt so tightly around his face that all you could see were his eyes and nose, making sure he would be hard to identify later. He was good. He darted his fingers into pockets and withdrew them deftly. No one felt a thing. But he came up empty handed every time. They had nothing to steal.

Nearby a man was hawking cigarettes. He wore a ring in his ear and the band of his broad-brimmed cowboy hat was a splash of bright feathers. The handle of a long-bladed knife protruded from his waistband. A few feet away, a group of men were tossing dice against a wall, throwing down cigarettes and nickels as bets. One man was betting nudie playing cards, which he withdrew carefully from a well-worn deck, kissed fondly, and tossed into the pot.

The room was filled with tobacco smoke and the noise of men talking and arguing and mumbling to themselves. We all waited.

Suddenly, the guards burst into the room. They slammed their cudgels on the chairs and shouted: "Everybody out! Everybody out!" No explanations were demanded and none were offered. The men shuffled out of the Big Room, into the processing area, and out through the swinging metal doors to the street.

One of the guards thrust his hand into the small of my back and shoved. My neck snapped back and I stumbled. "Get out!" he shouted. "Now!"

We had not been out in the street for more than five

minutes when two jackrollers pounced on a derelict. One of them threw a hammerlock around the man's neck and began to choke him while the other ripped a ring from his finger and rifled his pockets. Coins spilled on the sidewalk. One of the jackrollers stooped to pick them up, casually, one by one. The two of them sauntered off, slapping each other's palms and laughing. No one made a move to help. The man just slumped against the wall and stared at the sidewalk. No one said a word to him.

The shelter reopened at four. It had been closed, I learned, so it could be swabbed down with disinfectant. Once again I took my place on the line that formed in front of the glassed-in processing booth and waited to speak to the man behind the desk at Window 1. "How long is this going to take?" I wondered out loud.

The man in front of me turned around. He looked me up and down. "You're new," he said. It was not a question but a statement. I nodded. "Listen, young fella," he offered, "let me give you some advice. This is a bad place. You're better off taking your chances in the streets. You get out of here. And whatever you do, don't let them make you go to the Palace Hotel."

There were fewer than a hundred beds in the shelter then. Most men were sent to the six Bowery flophouses under contract with the city. The Palace, with its 500 beds, was the largest.

"Next." The bored voice came from behind the glass partition. I bent down so the clerk could hear me through the circle of holes in the glass barrier. He asked why I had come to the shelter. I told him I was an out-of-work gardener. "Came up from Pennsylvania. Couldn't find any work. Was sleeping in Grand Central until some guy told me about this place." He grunted and wrote down a case number—4953331—next to my name on a three-by-five card.

"Where do you want to stay?" he asked. I shrugged and he reached for a rubber stamp, pounded it on the card, and handed it to me through the slot. It was a ticket for meals at the Men's Shelter and a month's lodging. At the Palace Hotel.

"Dinner starts at five," the clerk told me. He made it sound like a warning.

I had about an hour to wait. I was making some notes in my little Woolworth book when a guard approached me. "What are you writing there?" he asked. He sounded friendly enough. "Poetry," I lied.

"Figures," he said. "You don't look like you belong. Poetry, huh?" He chuckled and shook his head, as if to say "Now I've seen it all." "I ever seen you around here?"

"First time."

"Take some advice, buddy. Don't stick around. Just get your shit grouped and get out of here. And don't trust nobody. There's guys here would kill their mothers just to go to the orphans' picnic. No joke."

The long, noisy chow line snaked from the Big Room to the basement mess hall. Most of the men were black and a surprising number seemed able-bodied. One of them, a short, powerfully built man in his forties, told me he had been living on the Bowery off and on for two years.

In the summer, he said, he worked as a caddy at an upstate golf course. "I do real good," he said. "But the truth of it is I just can't hang onto money. Spend it fast as I get it."

He said he hated the shelter. But he had no place else to go. He asked where I was staying.

"The Palace."

"You shouldn't have let them do that," he said, shaking his head violently. "White boy like you. No way. You see if you can't get yourself into a place like the Union on Hester Street. It's safe there. No boozin' allowed, no dope, no faggy stuff."

The cook reached across the steam table with a plate. On it, swimming in the water from a scattering of canned vegetables, was a glob of stuffing the size of a softball and a large, tough meatball. I grabbed two slices of Wonder Bread and two pats of butter from a stack on the counter, picked up a dish of prunes, and found a seat at one of the long mess hall tables.

A Rastafarian got up as I sat down. His hair was a nest of matted braids and he reeked. He left the table, scrounged through a garbage pail, and pulled out a Styrofoam cup. Silently, he brought it back to the table and began to cram his portion of stuffing into it. He packed it down tightly with the heel of his hand, then put it uncovered into the pocket of his street-filthy coat and left.

A heavyset black man in his forties took the Rastafarian's place. He screwed up his face and waved his hand in front of it to erase the odor. "Phew," he said. "Some people got no self-respect." He was dressed neatly in jeans and an Army fatigue jacket and he seemed out of place here. He nodded in greeting. "Mike," he said. I told him my name and we began to talk.

When he worked, Mike told me, he was a short-order cook. But work was hard to find. "Can't find a thing now," he said, "but I hope to go down to the Poconos in April."

I laughed. "The Poconos! Sure, and I'm gonna sail to the Riviera next week."

Mike smiled. "You're new, right? I can tell. You can see it. I don't know you, but my advice is that you listen more than you talk and you'll be okay. Just advice."

I felt chastened, and for a time neither of us spoke. Then Mike said, "See, when the weather starts getting good, they send in buses to take men from the Bowery to the Poconos and up to the Catskills to work the resorts. You know, dishwasher, laborer, whatever. Other times, you can go out to the island—Long Island, that is—and dig potatoes. Money's not bad if you can hold onto it. But they got the company store system out there. Sometimes you wind up owing *them* money."

He carefully buttered his bread, took a few bites, then looked back up at me. "You," he said. "You're strong and young. Don't you be waiting around here till April. You go get yourself a job, you hear? The Bowery is no place for a man to be."

I had come here because so many of the homeless men and women I had been talking with had told me they would rather be living in the streets than in the vermin-infested, crime-ridden, firetrap flophouses that the city had sent them to from the Men's Shelter. I found these stories difficult to believe—what could be worse than the streets?

The Bowery is a district of pawn shops, restaurant supply houses, used clothing shops, missions, dive saloons, and flophouses. For nearly a century its name has been synonymous with skid row. Men, their eyes glazed and veined red, their faces and arms pocked with unhealing sores, wander the streets as if in trances; some sprawl on sidewalks amid the shards of broken bottles. At Houston Street, the energetic ones arm themselves with buckets and sponges and swab motorists' windshields for a quarter. But most are too far gone even to extend their hands to beg.

Even on that cold February evening, I saw men without coats, some without shoes. The booze in their systems would lower their body temperature, making them more susceptible to hypothermia and frostbite, but they seemed beyond caring.

These alcoholics and drug addicts were the traditional denizens of the Bowery and of similar skid rows everywhere. But they were no longer typical of America's homeless. In numbers that were increasing by the hundreds daily, the homeless were battered women, jobless workers, spaced-out Vietnam veterans, the untreated mentally ill, and, simply, those who were just too poor to get by.

These—and not the reeling drunks—were the homeless that I was seeing daily on the streets, in parks and alleyways, in subways, dressed in rags and living out of shopping bags or battered luggage held together with rope.

Sociologists, who were just beginning to recognize and study the burgeoning problem, had set the number of homeless in New York at 36,000 and estimated that at least 6,000 of them were women. In every city in the country, there were thousands upon thousands more—experts were estimating as many as a quarter of a million people all told: enough to populate Des Moines.

In Pittsburgh, homeless men were sleeping in caves above the Allegheny River. In St. Louis, at least 200 families were reported to have taken over abandoned buildings because they had no place else to go. In Salt Lake City, men huddled in makeshift tent camps and compared stories of joblessness back home in Michigan and Pennsylvania, Washington and Indiana, Oregon and Illinois. In Washington, D.C., shopping bag ladies were hawking pencils on Pennsylvania Avenue and sleeping at night on benches in Lafayette Park across the street from the White House.

No accurate head count of the homeless was possible, but researchers, welfare workers, and government officials were beginning to compile an unofficial census. The numbers in the year Phyllis Iannotta died were staggering:

Atlanta—1,500
Baltimore—4,000
Chicago—8,000
Los Angeles—7,500
New York—36,000
Philadelphia—8,000
Pittsburgh—1,500
St. Louis—15,000
Seattle—5,000
Washington, D.C.—10,000

Since then, researchers believe, the numbers have doubled in many cities, and thousands more homeless remain unaccounted for in small cities and towns from coast to coast. Never before, not even during the Great Depression, have so many of our people been jettisoned into the streets. I was to get a brief taste of what life could be like for many of them.

The clerk at the Palace Hotel looked at me through the bullet-proof glass window of his little enclosed booth. He put down his copy of *Playboy*, took my ticket, and returned it to me with the number 570 written on the back. I waited. He waited. Then it dawned on him.

He laughed. "First time?" I nodded. He laughed again, a deep, knowing chuckle. "Five-seventy," he said. "That's your bed number. Fifth floor." He pushed a buzzer and the locked gate to the sleeping quarters swung open. He pointed upstairs, then turned back to his centerfold. I walked through the gate and it clanked shut behind me.

Once again the stench: the smell of sweat and failure. Men trudged listlessly past me across the dirty plank floors. Five-by-seven-foot sleeping cubicles, looking like row after row of grim cabanas, filled the first two stories. Each cubicle had room for a metal cot and no more. They had no ceilings but were covered with chicken wire to prevent people from throwing things into them. And they had doors. Robbery, assault, and knifings were common here. The day before, I would later learn, a man had been blinded at the Palace when someone threw lye in his face. Doors were important.

The cubicles were the luxury accommodations at the Palace Hotel. They were reserved for customers who could afford the $3.25 daily rate. As a lowly Men's Shelter "ticketman," I would have no such amenities.

I climbed the black metal stairs to the fifth-floor sleeping bays and pushed open swinging doors. My eyes had to adjust to the surreal gloom. The air was gray from tobacco smoke and seemed to hang in layers. Three uncovered eighty-watt bulbs provided the only light in the eighty-by-forty-foot room.

Rows of metal cots, two feet apart, filled the room. Beside each was a broken wall locker, its door sprung or ripped off altogether. Men lay on their beds, some of them fully dressed, others in their shorts. One, a skeleton of a man, was naked. He had no toes on his left foot. Another man snored loudly, an empty half pint of rye clutched to his breast; next to him a man sat on his bed, smoking a joint.

I walked around the room three times trying to find my bed. Finally, I spotted 570 scrawled in black Magic Marker on a battered olive-drab locker. My bed was next to it. A sheet, greasy and black with grime, and a thin, gray blanket were crumpled on the worn mattress. There was no pillow. I searched the bedding for bugs, but it was too dark to see if the bed was infested.

It was 10:30. I decided to postpone the inevitable.

Downstairs, in the first-floor common room, about 100 men were sitting on vinyl-backed kitchen chairs, smoking and gazing up at the color TV bolted to the wall.

A young man, tall and painfully thin with close-cropped hair and a worn, emaciated face, was talking loudly to himself in a language only he seemed to understand. The bearded old man next to him paid no attention. Bent almost in half at the waist, he was busily combing the floor with his hand for cigarette butts. He found one, picked it up, lit it, and heaved a sigh of contentment.

Across the room a young Pakistani, his shirt torn and stained with blood, rummaged through a trash can. He pulled up a crust of bread and gnawed on it hungrily.

At the far end of the long, narrow room half a dozen muscular young men, many of them tattooed and wearing bandannas like latter-day pirates, stood ominously against the wall, a menacing stag line. Their eyes fastened on everyone, and everyone seemed careful not to return their stares. Jackrollers.

At eleven, a muscular guard reached up and switched off the TV. "No more. Off the floor," he chanted. The men trooped out of the room and trudged up the metal stairs in single file, silently and in slow motion.

I climbed along with them to the fifth floor, but sat on the stairs outside the sleeping bay, unwilling to face my filthy bed. Men continued to walk up the stairs past me. Their eyes bore the vacant, fatigued look of soldiers after a long battle.

After the line had passed and disappeared behind the swinging dormitory door, a young, slim boy in tight black toreador pants with a lavender scarf around his neck sashayed up the stairs, stopped in front of me, and posed. His mouth was accented with a garish smear of red lipstick. "Wanna get friendly, white boy?" He rubbed his hand obscenely over his crotch. "I'd like to get a little piece of you." He flexed his arms, revealing knotted biceps, then pushed past me menacingly without waiting for an answer.

Moments later, a blubbery black man emerged from the dormitory in boxer shorts. "Got a cigarette?"

I gave him one from my pack of Pall Malls. He took it and disappeared back behind the swinging door without a word. But I heard him chortling to his friends: "Christ, he actually *gave* me a butt. Gave it to me!" A burst of laughter erupted. Then, suddenly, he pushed open the door and poked out his head. "Say, where are you sleeping?" His tone was friendly, ingratiating.

"Five-seventy," I answered. The moment the words left my mouth I knew I'd done a dumb thing. My near-full pack of cigarettes was worth at least $2 at the dime-apiece Bowery exchange rate, and that was more than the price of a pint of Midnight Express.

I sat alone on the stairs until midnight, when the night watchman, a derelict in tattered clothes with a time clock slung over his shoulder, found me there pretending to read a newspaper.

"What the hell do you think you're doing?" he demanded. "I mean, just who the hell do you think you are?" His voice amplified from a shrill whine to a pitch just short of a scream. "You get your ass in that room and get into bed." He was ancient, toothless, and harmless; there was little he could have done if I'd refused. But I let him hustle me through the door. He stood over me, waiting, until I lay down on my bunk, fully clothed.

I pulled my cap down over my ears, pulled up the collar of my overcoat, and buttoned it around my throat. I was thankful for the three layers of clothing between me and that filthy mattress. Most of the men were already asleep, except for the cigarette man who sat at the edge of his bed facing me, watching.

I looked at my watch. It was three o'clock in the morning. Somewhere in the room a radio played softly. The room was quiet, almost tranquil. But the sleeping figures tossed and turned fitfully, some of them waking with hacking coughs. I tried to stay awake.

Then, out of the corner of my eye, I saw a tiny, grayish-brown bug crawl up my sleeve and across the lapel of my coat. I flicked it off. Then a second bug marched up my sleeve. I flicked that off, too. Another took its place. Bedbugs.

I tried to be nonchalant. But the presence of those tiny insects, each not much bigger than the point of a pencil, made my flesh creep. Slowly I pulled myself up from the bunk and walked calmly to the well-lighted bathroom, where I ripped off the coat and held it in front of me at arm's length. It was crawling with bugs.

40

I wanted to rampage through the building, trashing bunks and wall lockers. I wanted to kick some ass. I marched noisily down the stairs, almost praying for someone to get in my way, slammed through the gates, and burst out of the Palace Hotel into the cold and lonesome night.

I longed to rip off the vermin-infested coat, but it was too cold. The digital readout over a bank building in the distance flashed 15 degrees. I could feel the bugs crawling all over my body. Fierce red welts formed on my neck and arms. They burned and itched mercilessly.

I was disgusted by them, disgusted by myself. I noticed that I was talking to myself, aloud. I felt like a pariah. I couldn't go home like that, all covered with bugs. Where could I go? I was confused, disoriented.

I walked block after block, trying to sort things out, trying to understand my rage, my confusion, knowing that I was overreacting. Yet I felt what I felt. I *was* angry. And I was humiliated. It made me sick from the inside out.

I walked for hours on the deserted streets, and eventually, like a moth drawn to light, I wound up in the neon brightness of Times Square, miles from the Bowery. I spent one of my three dollars for admission to an all-night porno joint, and behind the closed door of a peep show booth I removed my coat and examined it in the flickering light of the projector. The bugs were gone. But it made no difference now. I was tired and hungry and worn down.

Dawn was breaking when I finally summoned the will to go home. Upstairs, my wife and daughter were still asleep. I stepped inside, stripped off my clothes, threw them outside in a heap on the stoop, and climbed the stairs naked. I stood for a long time scrubbing myself in the shower.

The next day, the bites still itched as I sat in the office

of Robert Trobe, the city bureaucrat in charge of the shelters. I did not tell him where I had been the night before. Instead I let him tell me how well the city shelters were run and what a good place, all things considered, the Palace Hotel was, how the management cooperated with the city, how they ran a clean, safe place and changed the linens every day.

The three-by-five card the clerk gave me at the Men's Shelter is worn gray now. It is frayed at the edges and permanently creased from scores of foldings and refoldings. I carry it in my wallet to remember.

As I left Sister Nancy at the Dwelling Place on that August afternoon in 1981, I pulled out the card and examined it. It brought back the memory of what had been for me a single day's degradation. For Phyllis Iannotta, I knew, humiliation had been a condition of daily life for years.

Pieces
of Paper

"Phyllis?" The priest leaned back in his chair, closed his eyes, and joined his fingertips, meditatively making a church of his hands. "Oh yes, I knew Phyllis. She was quite a lady. She was a regular here, came to the church almost every day. Sometimes she'd spend five, six hours on the steps, sitting and smoking and watching people go by. She liked to keep an eye on things, you might say. Then she'd come inside, pray, say the stations, maybe go sit in a back pew and get some sleep for a while."

An imposing man, gray-haired with the muscular arms and barrel chest of an athlete, Father Robert Rappleyea was the pastor of Holy Cross Church, an anchor of respectability balanced on the border between Times Square and Hell's Kitchen. He had been Phyllis's priest for the last year or so of her life and had performed the last rites over her body in the parking lot behind the Dwelling Place.

43

The hard-backed chair he was sitting in seemed too small for his large frame, as did the squat maple writing table between us. The oak-paneled rectory room, illuminated only by the light from a small stained-glass window, was in somber contrast to the cleric's energetic presence.

"We get many people from the streets here," he said. "It is a safe place, a haven. They can come here to pray or be alone or to sleep in the pews. These poor people get little sleep, you know. They are constantly troubled, hassled, afraid. I am glad this is a place they can feel safe. I try to listen to their problems and to help them as best I can."

Rappleyea remembered that once he had given Phyllis his phone number and told her to call him "if ever she needed me and couldn't get to the church." That same phone number is in the pockets and purses of many Times Square people—hookers and bag ladies, runaways, alcoholics, and junkies.

"They are all part of our community," the gray-haired priest said. "Phyllis was part of our family. She was a regular, a communicant. She'd take her meals here sometimes, too. We have a feeding program for the needy on Saturdays. Nothing elaborate, mind you, just tuna sandwiches, hot soup, simple things like that, but we manage to feed about 200 people a week, sometimes more.

"Phyllis came here for clothing, too, about four times a year, for a change of seasons. She always picked out dark-colored slacks and for some reason she'd wear them with one leg rolled up." He laughed. "Could never figure that out."

Outside, the rush of traffic, the squealing of brakes, the blare of horns were reminders that beyond this sanctuary was Times Square, the epitome of everything this church opposed.

The priest seemed to read my thoughts. "This area is a real garbage pail," he said, shaking his head. "It is a sad, degrading place, probably the ugliest block in the world. Every social problem known to man is here and magnified: alcoholism, drug abuse, sexual perversion, crime, poverty. You name it, you see it here—the teenage hookers on Eighth Avenue, the runaways, the young homosexual hustlers, the porno shops, the peep shows, the head shops—sad, awful places, sad, awful people that remind us of how spiritually impoverished we have become, how we have lost our regard for womankind, for the family, for the Church . . ."

Rappleyea spoke with an energy that left little room for interruption.

"This must have been extremely difficult, this environment, for Phyllis," he continued. "She seemed to have been very committed to the old values, to church and home." He paused to gather his thoughts.

"You know, she could be very tough, very streetwise. She spoke this rough Brooklynese and every once in a while things got too much for her and she'd let loose with a string of four-letter words." He laughed. "In fact she'd go bananas, as the kids say. But as tough as she was, she was always well-mannered and showed a great deal of respect for me, for the priesthood. She was almost old-fashioned in that respect." Rappleyea shook his head and shrugged. "You don't see much of that anymore," he said.

"Phyllis was a very good person. Sure, she'd feel sorry for herself sometimes. But she always seemed to be more concerned about others. She wanted to make sure everybody got a fair shake. If she knew someone was in need, she'd make a point to come and tell us. Phyllis was very concerned about others. Take her brother, for example, she was very concerned about him . . ."

"A brother?" I asked. "She had a brother?" I hadn't known Phyllis had any family. "Is he still alive?"

A tired look came over Rappleyea's face. "Alive? Oh yes, Philip is alive, although he is killing himself slowly with alcohol. That's how I came to know him. Phyllis was very worried about his drinking. He was drunk all the time, unable to work, living in the subways, dragging himself through life an hour at a time.

"About a month before she was killed," Rappleyea continued, "Phyllis came to me and asked wouldn't I please talk to her brother about his drinking and see if I couldn't get him to go to a hospital for his eyes—he could hardly see and he had to have an operation. Well, Phyllis brought him here two, maybe three, times. But he wasn't interested in my help or anyone else's. I'm afraid he will always be that way."

The priest seemed to be struggling not to feel contempt. "Phyllis was a very strong person, lots of moral fiber," he said. "Her brother is very weak. I wouldn't be surprised that he was the cause of many of her problems."

He glanced at his watch, then heaved himself out of his hard-backed chair. "I really must be going," he said. "I have a funeral to go to. I don't know how much help I've been . . ."

"Her brother," I said. "How can I find him?"

Rappleyea shrugged. "In the streets, I suppose. He hangs out in this area, in Times Square. You should look for him there. His last name is Gennaro. I don't know why it's different from hers. I never got a straight answer from him on that score. I understand he uses the street name Popeye. Ask around, he's bound to turn up sooner or later . . ."

Binky's shoeshine stand had been at the corner of 42nd Street and Eighth Avenue in the middle of Times Square's "Minnesota Strip" for as long as I could remember: a red-vinyl armchair elevated on a three-foot wooden platform with ancient brass foot supports shaded by an old hot-dog-stand umbrella.

A wizened black man who covered his shaved head, winter and summer, rain or shine, with the same old brown watchman's cap, Binky was a constant in the daily anarchy of Times Square. Tall and slim, with strong, permanently stained hands, he held court daily amid a clutter of Kiwi tins and bottles of liquid boot polish. His stand was a gathering place for the Times Square elite—the tipsters and dopesters, the monte players, the pimps and their ladies. It was more than a hangout. It was a numbers drop, a message center, the first station on the Times Square grapevine.

"What can I do you for?" Binky asked as I fit my feet into the brass supports. His voice sounded as if his vocal cords had been run through a meat grinder.

"I'm looking for somebody," I said.

Binky chuckled. "Seems like ever'body's lookin' for somebody these days . . . blondes, brunets, pretty little café au lait girl on the stroll around the corner."

"Thanks, Binky, not this time. I'm looking for a man."

"Ooooeeeee!" Binky rolled his eyes until all you could see were the whites. "A man is it? Well, have you tried downstairs at Show World? Lots of men down there, all the boys a fella could want." He rubbed his fingers into the black polish and slapped them onto the tips of my shoes. He was enjoying his little game. "What you into anyway, my man? How can Binky be of assistance?"

"Like I said, I'm looking for a man—Philip Gennaro. They call him Popeye. He's maybe in his fifties or sixties. A white guy. Been on the streets for a while. Do you know him?"

Binky said nothing as he cracked the buffing rag rhythmically over my shoe. He stepped back to admire his work, then began on the next shoe. "Why you lookin' for him?" he asked. "He owe you money?"

"I only want to talk to him. About his sister. She was murdered last week. A shopping bag lady. You remember?"

"Yes, indeed I do. That one made the papers."

I smiled. "I just need some information from him, the kind only her brother could provide."

He tapped my foot. "That's it, chief. You can hit the street. Binky done your feet."

I stepped down and handed Binky a ten-dollar bill and a card with my phone number. "Put out the word, okay?"

Binky nodded. "I hear anything, I'll let you know."

Days passed, then weeks. The pope was shot; hunger strikers died in Maze Prison; Gary Gilmore was executed by firing squad; inflation dropped below 10 percent; a berserk motorist killed four on a sidewalk in Times Square; David Hinckley put a bullet in President Reagan; terrorists exploded bombs at the U.S. Mission and the Port Authority Bus Terminal; the Bing Crosby estate was set at $150 million . . .

I was in the middle of writing a story on deadline when the phone rang. I picked it up. "This is Tom LeCarver," the voice said. "I hear you're looking for Popeye." It took a moment for the name to register. "Yes, Popeye," I said. "I sure am. Did Binky tell you to call?"

"Binky?" the man said. "I don't know any Binky. The word is out you're looking for Popeye. Well, he's here— Kilroy's bar on Sixth Avenue between 42nd and 43rd. I'm the bartender. Popeye, he comes in every night around nine. Any time after that till closing time and you'll find him."

Kilroy's is one of those too-bright Irish shot-and-a-beer joints that reek of stale booze and soggy corned beef. The place was filled with office workers, hard hats, and Times Square drifters. At one end of the bar a brassy, middle-aged blonde allowed a boy half her age to paw her ample bosom in exchange for orange blossoms.

Phyllis's brother was sitting on a bar stool, his head resting in the palm of his hand, which was connected by his elbow to the long wooden bar. A faded blue tattoo of a heart pierced by a dagger peered from under the rolled-up sleeve of his gray work shirt. His legs were short and bowed, and they dangled from the bar stool like a child's from a church pew. He appeared to be asleep.

I knew it was him: the bulbous nose, the muscular forearms, the tattoo, the bandy legs. Popeye. The name fit him like a glove.

I approached cautiously. "Popeye?"

No answer.

I tried again. "Are you Popeye?" I asked. "Are you Philip Gennaro?"

Again no answer. But the old man opened his eyes and I could see him watching me suspiciously in the dirty mirror behind the bar.

"Who wants to know?" The mumbled challenge seemed to come as an afterthought. The old man had decided to talk.

"I do," I said. "What are you drinking?" Those were the magic words. The old man swiveled on his stool and faced me. He nodded to the bartender, who measured out a shot of rye and spilled it into a tall glass of ginger ale in front of him. I asked for a draft beer.

"I'm a reporter," I said. "I want to talk to you about your sister." He shook his head as if to clear it. "My sister," he said, "was a shopping bag lady. She is dead." He took a sip of his drink and propped his tired gray head in his hand. He closed his eyes, and I thought he was going to fall asleep again.

I put my hand on his shoulder. "Popeye, I want to know about Phyllis. Tell me about when you were kids."

Silence.

I nudged him again. "Popeye?"

He opened his eyes. "Red Hook," he said. "We was kids in Red Hook, Brooklyn." He stared into his drink as if it were a crystal ball. He seemed to be trying to look into the past, but acted as if it were too painful—not the memories themselves, but the effort of remembering.

"One-eighteen Sullivan Street," he said after a time. "That's where I was born. One-eighteen Sullivan Street, Red Hook." His voice was thick with the accents of Brooklyn, and his tongue seemed weighted by a lifetime of heavy drinking. I had to strain to make out what he was saying. Every syllable—and he didn't use many—was work to him.

"How about school," I tried. "Where did Phyllis go to school? You remember where your sister went to school, don't you?"

"I . . . I don't remember," he said. "That was a long time ago."

I was beginning to lose my patience. "Well, what about you, Phil. Where'd you go to school?"

No answer. "Philip?"

"Huh?"

"I asked you where you went to school."

"Oh, yeah. I dunno. P.S. 36, P.S. 38, I'm not sure. That was a long time ago."

"You must remember something about your childhood, Phil. Just tell me about when you were a kid, okay?"

"We was poor," he said, "real poor." He stared at himself in the mirror behind the bar. His face was seamed with deep, dark lines, like a china cup that had been broken and badly repaired. "My father," he began, "he had a push-cart . . . junk . . . we never had much. But he was an honest man, worked hard all his life."

Popeye fell silent and I was about to prompt him, when he spoke again. "He was a cook in the Italian army, from Napoli. My sister, she was born there."

"In Naples?"

"Yeah, on the other side."

"Did you speak Italian at home?"

"Yeah, Neapolitan. They couldn't speak good American. My father—his name was Michele Iannotta—he spoke broken. My mother—Carmella Monica Iannotta was her name—spoke a little, not much."

"How come your name is different?"

Philip looked at me as if that were none of my business. "I just started using it, that's all."

I pressed. "Why?"

"It sounds the same."

"Sounds the same?" I laughed. "Iannotta. Gennaro. They don't sound the same to me. So how come you changed your name? You adopted or something?"

He gave me a menacing glare. "No, I was not adopted or something. I just changed my name, that's all."

"When?" I asked.

"When I was at Mount Loretto," he said.

"Mount Loretto? Where's that?"

Popeye drained his glass. He struggled to get off the stool and still keep his balance. "I gotta go now," he said, and staggered out of the bar.

When I met Philip Gennaro a week later, he was sitting in the same place at the bar in Kilroy's, slumped over a drink. By then I had learned that Mount Loretto was a reform school on Staten Island. I also had learned that Phyllis's brother had been born Philip Iannotta on June 6, 1922, but that by 1939 he had become Philip Gennaro, convicted felon, in the records of the New York State Department of Corrections.

"Oh, yeah," Popeye said. "I been in 'em all. Yessir, I done a lot of time—Napanoch, Dannemora, Elmira, Sing Sing. Burglary, grand larceny auto. All hard time." He rolled up his shirt sleeve and pointed to the tattoo on his right forearm: The heart, pierced by a dagger, was surrounded by garlands. Under it was the name Fay.

"She come and seen me every time I got sent up. Except for Dannemora. Cost too much to go way up there. But she wanted to anyway."

"Girlfriend?" I asked.

"No, no, no," he said impatiently. "Fay. That was the name I gave my sister. A nickname, like they say. I gave it to her when we was kids. She liked it when I called her that. That was *my* name for her."

Philip lifted his head and looked at me directly for the first time. His eyes were watery and I couldn't tell if it was from the booze or tears. "She was always there when I needed her," he said. "Always, even when we was kids in Red Hook . . ." He took a few short sips from his glass. "We'd fight back to back. I mean fight. She was always a fighter. Tough, too. She'd stand up for me. I was her kid brother, you know. She always did right by me."

He drained his glass and started to get off the bar stool. "Last time I saw her was right here, just a couple days before it happened . . . before she was, you know, murdered." He gestured toward a red Leatherette booth. "We sat right over there. She had anisette and quinine water, if you can believe that. She wasn't what you'd call a drinker. Now and then, maybe, that's all. She gave me twenty bucks. She said she was gonna get a place real soon, so I could move in with her like I done a lot of times before."

I asked Popeye where he and his sister had lived, but his answer was typically vague. "Lotsa different places," he said. "I can't remember. I got her papers. It's all in there. I can't tell you no more. You can have her papers. I got 'em at the bookstore. C'mon." He turned abruptly and began to walk out—half swagger, half stagger—toward Sixth Avenue. I settled his tab and quickly caught up with him. "I got her stuff in the bookstore," he repeated. "You can have it. It's yours."

Popeye walked the one and a half blocks to the One-Forty Bookstore like a horse on its way to the stable: swiftly and purposefully, as if his feet landed in exactly the same places every time he made the trip.

"Hey, hey, Popeye, How ya doin'?" The man on the high stool behind the cash register greeted Philip like a long-lost friend. About a dozen customers, all of them men, most of them in business suits, were browsing through the store.

53

I scanned the titles: *Mary Learns How, The Bed for Bread Girls, Diary of a Teenage Nymph.*

Men flipped the pages of magazines filled with photos of naked teenagers as pert and blonde as their own daughters—or sons—back home in the suburbs. They eyed each other furtively as they moved from rack to rack or read the absurdly lurid blurbs on the peep show booths—"Two slick chicks give up their boyfriends for life on the farm. Both make it with a 500-pound pig"—before slipping behind the door.

There was a little something here for every bizarre taste: artificial penises a yard long, French ticklers, creams, ointments, gels, and pills promising every sort of aphrodisiac pleasure, leather goods with bedeviling studs and straps, and "life-size" inflatable mannequins with gaping rubber mouths.

Downstairs real-life mannequins—bored and barely more lifelike than their air-filled counterparts—gyrated on a carpeted stage to a mind-numbing disco beat.

"Joe," Popeye told the counterman, "this guy's writin' about my sister Fay." He added proudly: "I'm helpin' him out." He disappeared to find the papers he'd promised.

"Joe Quagliano," the counterman said, extending a hand, "good to meet ya." He was tall and wiry with dark hair and narrow-set eyes. He gave my hand a firm squeeze. "You're taking good care of our friend Popeye, right? Givin' him a little somethin' for his trouble?"

I nodded.

"See," Quagliano continued, "Popeye is sort of the mascot around here. Tony, he's the owner, he sort of took pity on him and lets him sleep nights on the couch in the dancers' dressing room downstairs in exchange for sweeping up and running errands. It's just a little room, all cluttered up with makeup all over the place, costumes, stockings, you know, all kinds of feminine things." He laughed. "And maybe some beer cans or a hypodermic syringe. Some of the girls, well, you know . . ."

"Yeah," I said. "I know."

"Popeye does things for the girls and they tip him. He might make, oh, I guess maybe five, ten bucks a day. Of course, all that goes for booze. So he can always use a little help and we try to look out for him."

Popeye returned with a nine-by-twelve-inch brown paper bag. "This is it," he said, "all her stuff." The bag was sealed tightly with Scotch tape, and on it were printed the words "I Love New York." It contained all that was left of the things that had come in and out of Phyllis Iannotta's life in sixty-seven years.

Late that night, while my wife and five-year-old daughter slept in the adjoining rooms, I peeled the Scotch tape from the bag and spilled its contents onto my desk. All told there were only sixty-four pieces of paper. They provided the first tentative brush strokes in the portrait of Phyllis Iannotta and a clue to how she became homeless.

A computer-printed Supplemental Security Income Notice of Planned Action stated "Beginning April 1980 the amount due you will be reduced." The form was dated the last day of February 1980. Nowhere did it explain why Phyllis's entitlement was being cut. But it meant that instead of receiving $315 a month in combined retirement and disability payments, Phyllis would receive only $291.41.

Another form letter in the "I Love New York" bag, this

one from the management of the Times Square Motor Hotel on West 43rd Street dated two days earlier, stated: "Due to increased operating costs, we are compelled to raise your rent from $162 to $177." The letter was addressed only to the Occupant of Room 1226. It meant that after paying her rent Phyllis would be left with just $114.41 a month—or less than four dollars a day—to live on.

Still another form, a New York State Department of Social Services form 2274 dated March 18, 1980, revealed the results: "Client is an SSI recipient who is out of funds," it said, "and is in dire need of food. . . . She is disabled."

But nothing, apparently, was done. The rent receipts from the Times Square Motor Hotel, all held together neatly with a rubber band, ended at July 1980. After that, Phyllis's home had become the streets.

Also in the brown paper bag, as if to counterbalance the harsh forms, were four religious tracts, prayer cards from three Catholic churches, a booklet of inspirational poems and a pamphlet beseeching Padre Pio ("The ONLY priest," the pamphlet proclaimed, "ever to receive the stigmata") to "Please pray for me, ever endeavoring to follow your simple life, to accept the Crosses, to move forward, not fearful of suffering, resigning one's self to God's will in all things, thankful for the joys and blessings and the graces, the failures and the sorrows received, to do penance in various ways and also works of mercy, as reparations for my sins. . . ."

What sins, I wondered as I slipped the papers back in the bag, could Phyllis Iannotta have committed that she had suffered for them as she did?

As much as the contents of that brown paper bag told me about how Phyllis wound up on the streets and about the faith that sustained her there, I learned more from what wasn't there: no photographs, no letters, no address books, no money, no mementos. None of the things most of us spend lifetimes collecting. Possessions, *things.* They fill our attics and our basements, our pockets and our purses and our bureau drawers. But to have things, you have to have a place to put them. You have to have a home.

I went into my daughter's bedroom, a room cluttered with dolls and toys and things, and I watched as her back rose and fell with the deep breathing of childhood sleep. On the floor next to her was a book, *The Attic of the Wind.* I had read it to her only a few hours before. It is a charming book about where all the things we lose really go. I picked it up, and by the soft glow of the night light I began to read:

> *"Yes, the Attic of the Wind can store*
> *All the world's treasure, and even more . . .*
> *The handkerchief you forgot to hold,*
> *The spelling paper with the star of gold,*
> *The picture you drew for Mother's Day. . . ."*

That night I dreamed of my daughter. She was sitting in the middle of a large, grassy meadow wearing her favorite dress, a frilly red calico. All around her were shopping bags brimming with brightly colored bits of cloth and paper, which she pulled out and tossed gaily into the air. Poof! They vanished as she giggled in delight. Phyllis had been a little girl once, too, with a favorite dress and toys and things. Where had they all gone? What had gone wrong?

John Huber, the manager of the Times Square Motor Hotel, seemed strangely out of place in his surroundings, dressed as he was in a blue suit and crisply starched white shirt.

Outside his neat office, perhaps half a dozen of the residents of the hotel, most of them elderly and all of them poor, sat in chairs in the marbled lobby staring into space, waiting for the day to end. An old woman in pink house slippers padded slowly across the floor, pausing at each painful step. A uniformed guard stood in a corner, his eyes glazed with boredom. The whole place seemed to groan under the weight of its own shabbiness.

But Huber was as bright and businesslike as if he were in charge of the St. Moritz. I showed him the rent receipts from the "I Love New York" bag. "Do you remember her?" I asked. "A little woman with salt and pepper hair and thick glasses." Huber shook his head. He delved into a filing cabinet and withdrew a small dossier.

"I see from our records that Miss Iannotta stayed here from February 8, 1979 until, let's see . . ." He riffled through a stack of old invoices. "Yes, until July 15, 1980. She had room 1226 and she was paying $177 a month at the time she left."

I asked Huber if he thought the February rent increase might have had anything to do with her departure. "Oh, I really couldn't say," he said. "This is a hotel after all. People come and go. It's none of our business why. I will say this though." He looked up as if to confide a deep secret. "It could have been a factor. I'm sorry to say that it did create some hardship for our guests on public assistance. It's not fair, not right. But what can *we* do?"

Huber sighed. "It was not always like this," he said. "This was once a top-of-the-line luxury hotel." He pointed to the pictures on his office wall. They were artists' renderings from the 1950s of the Times Square Motor Hotel. The interior views were tinted in pleasing pastels; the exteriors showed the hotel as the backdrop of a Times Square I had never known—clean and bright and filled with strollers, all of them white and all of them smiling as if they didn't have a care in the world.

"This is what it was like before Mayor Lindsay decided New York would be Fun City," Huber said. He spat out the phrase as if it had burned his tongue. "From then on it was all downhill—hookers, peep shows, the whole dirty mess. Tourists were afraid to stay in this neighborhood. And who could blame them? Our business declined very quickly. The whole midtown hotel industry was in serious trouble. That's when we decided to take permanents. We didn't have much choice if we wanted to survive."

He shrugged philosophically. "Of course, that meant we had to lower or standards a bit, take welfare people, even some bag ladies, people like your Miss Iannotta. It was a shame what happened to her. I read all about it in the paper. I wish I could place her in my mind, but you know how it is, in this business you don't remember the quiet ones."

Huber rose from his desk. "Is there anything more I can do for you?" he asked. I told him I would like to see Phyllis's old room. He looked at his register. The room was vacant. "I don't suppose it could do any harm," he said, and he summoned the expressionless guard to take me to room 1226.

The guard unlocked the door and pushed it open. He hadn't spoken a word on the jerky elevator ride to the twelfth floor, and he stood silently outside the room as I entered. A twin bed lay lengthwise against one wall, nearly filling the tiny room. It was covered with a pink chenille spread that clashed violently with the bright vermilion carpet and gold-on-beige floral wallpaper.

A cheap Masonite dresser leaned unsteadily against the opposite wall. Above it was a colorful print, an autumn woodland scene, hung in a fake-wood frame. There was a tiny porcelain sink and a small closet with hangers on the rack that rattled when I opened the door.

An armchair, its orange vinyl upholstery torn in places, stood in a corner by the room's lone window. I sat in it and looked out across the rooftops of Fun City and tried to imagine what Phyllis had been like, what she had looked like, in this tiny room. What, I wondered, had Phyllis hung on those rattling hangers? What *things* had she kept here in the months that this had been her home? And what had happened to them? All I could picture was the battered corpse that lay on the black asphalt parking lot in Hell's Kitchen.

Half an hour later and two blocks away, I sat in the office of Mike Pregon, assistant manager of the midtown Manhattan bureau of the Social Security Administration, and surveyed Times Square from the huge plate-glass window in the corner of his office at 1515 Broadway. The view was pretty much the same. But the image that emerged of Phyllis was very different.

"Oh yes, I remember Miss Iannotta," Pregon said. "She used to come in every month for her checks—she got regular Social Security and SSI—and, ah, well," he searched for a tactful phrase, "she wasn't easy to forget. She, ah, sort of made her presence known. You see, she could be very loud, particularly when she wanted her own way. You could hear her yelling from one end of the floor to the other."

Pregon apologized. "I'm afraid I can't tell you much more about her—hundreds and hundreds of people come through this office every week, and, as you can imagine, I can't familiarize myself with the details of all their cases. But I'm sure you'll find some useful information in this." He patted a thick brown folder in front of him and slid it across the desk. It was marked IANNOTTA, FILOMENA. I opened the file. On the top was a long, green application for a Social Security card. It was dated February 3, 1938, only three years after Franklin Roosevelt had created the program. It was the middle of the Great Depression, and Phyllis was twenty-three years old.

Here, in a two-inch-thick dossier compiled over more than four decades by the bureaucracy that has compiled files on more than 285 million Americans—more than the FBI, more even than the IRS—was the history of Phyllis Iannotta. It began with a photostat of a document stamped in three places with the impressive seals of the municipality of Santa Maria Capua Vetere noting the birth of one Filomena Iannotta, *un bambino sesso femminile*, to Michele Iannotta, thirty-nine, a peasant farmer, and the former Carmella Monica, a housewife, at 10:30 P.M. on the eighth day of May 1914.

Under it, in long, bureaucratic forms with numbers, was the outline of a life: from a little town near Naples to Ellis Island, to the democratizing schoolyards of New York; then the fight to survive the Depression, followed by World War II and long hours on an assembly line at the Brooklyn Navy Yard at $6.16 a day.

After the war, the records revealed year after year of hard work at low pay in factories and offices throughout the

61

city. Forty employers over twenty-two years: Emerson Radio & Phonograph Co. on Eighth Avenue in Manhattan, F. W. Woolworth Co. on Broadway, Lutheran Medical Center on 55th Street in Brooklyn, the New York City Board of Education, the Quaker Maid Co. on Lexington Avenue, and others.

The documents revealed every dime of her earnings—from the $5.22 Esquire Radio Corp. paid her for a brief stint in 1953 to the $3,320 she received from Lutheran Medical Center in 1968, her best year. But they gave few hints of exactly what it was she did. Just ordinary jobs, most likely, working among ordinary people in ordinary places. The kind most Americans come home from every night.

Phyllis began to emerge as an independent woman, a woman who had never married, had never had children, had always supported herself. Hidden in her dossier was a story of struggle and sacrifice, of how she had managed, slowly, to improve her lot, moving up from Red Hook, one of the poorest and toughest neighborhoods in all New York, to Brooklyn's Sunset Park, then to Bensonhurst and eventually settling in solidly middle-class Bay Ridge in the mid-1950s.

Then, in 1969, her earnings plummeted to only $369. The records indicate that she worked only three months that year and that she never worked more than three months a year after that, at least not on the books. By the mid-1970s, it appeared that Phyllis had stopped working altogether. A form at the end of the dossier offered a possible explanation. It was an application for disability insurance benefits. In Block 4, under "What Is Your Disability?", Phyllis had written, "Mental condition." It was dated October 5, 1979—just a day after other papers showed she had been released from South Beach Psychiatric Center on Staten Island. She had been a patient there for one month, according to the dossier. The diagnosis: paranoid schizophrenia.

All these papers, all these printed forms with their neat little blanks. They told so much, and yet so very little— just enough to provide a label: immigrant, working woman, old maid, madwoman, bag lady. They told *what* Phyllis was, but not *who*.

I needed to know Phyllis Iannotta, who she had been, where she had come from, what had happened to her. I needed to know for my own sake and for the sake of my daughter, who was growing up in a real world where losses aren't recovered in the Attic of the Wind.

In my mind's eye I saw a little dark-haired girl, skipping rope on a Brooklyn sidewalk more than sixty years ago, free of care, with no thought of what the future might bring, with no worry greater than that she might miss the rhythm of the rope as it slapped its hypnotic beat on the pavement:

> *"Lady, lady, turn around,*
> *Lady, lady, touch the ground,*
> *Lady, lady, touch your shoe,*
> *Lady, lady, twenty-three skiddoo . . ."*

There was no hint of her in the two inches of official records and the sixty-four pieces of paper in the "I Love New York" bag. But I knew that she must have existed.

Dusty
Notebooks,
Faded
Memories

May 9, 1915 must have been a day of celebration aboard
the SS *Stampalia*. For even in the stench of the steerage
decks, a child's first birthday could not have passed un-
noticed. Three days out at sea, Filomena Iannotta completed her first year of life as the steamer pitched and rolled
toward Ellis Island.

Government researchers found her name for me on mi-
crofilm copies of the ship's manifest preserved in the National Archives, along with the manifests of all the ships
that brought immigrants to New York between 1897 and
1942. More than 326,700 men, women, and children passed
through Ellis Island in 1915 alone, but thanks to an index
prepared by the Works Progress Administration during the
Depression, the search for Filomena Iannotta took only a
few hours.

The long, narrow document, filled with row after row of names in precise Edwardian script, placed Carmella Iannotta and her baby on a page with the Cecoria family, the Gaulier family, the DeRocchis, the Guafrocchis, the Rufos, and more than thirty others. All told, more than 2,000 immigrants had been crowded into steerage aboard the 9,000-ton *Stampalia* to make the transatlantic voyage.

From the manifest I learned that Carmella Iannotta was a twenty-eight-year-old housewife, four feet nine, and in good health. The detailed sheets indicated that Michele Iannotta had made the same voyage a year earlier, that he had put up the money for his family's sixteen-day voyage, and that he was waiting for them—for his wife and the daughter he had never seen—at 157 Connover Street in a place called Brooklyn.

It was a dangerous voyage. There was a war on in Europe and the waters were infested with submarines. The *Stampalia* had been at sea only two days when the *Lusitania* was sunk off the coast of Ireland; a year later the *Stampalia* itself would be torpedoed and sent to the bottom by a German U-boat. But there were more immediate hazards: severe overcrowding, filth, sickness.

On the shelves of the library at the Center for Migration Studies on Staten Island, I found a U.S. Senate Immigration Committee report from 1911 in which shocked investigators described the kind of conditions Carmella Iannotta and her *bambino sesso femminile* must have endured to begin a new life in a new land:

"The sleeping quarters are large compartments, accommodating as many as 300 or more persons each. . . . The berths are in two tiers with two feet and six inches of space above each. They consist of an iron framework containing a mattress, a pillow, or more often a life preserver as a substitute, and a blanket. The mattress and the pillow, if there is one, are filled with straw or seaweed. On some lines this is renewed every trip. . . ."

The compartments were cold and damp, with exposed pipes that frequently leaked on the berths. Blankets were so thin as to be virtually useless. "Generally," the report noted, "the passengers retire almost fully dressed to keep warm."

There were no storage lockers or hooks for clothing so that each berth was littered "by every possession that the passenger could not wear or carry continually on his person." Yet, one of the investigators crossing with the immigrants reported, the berth was the passenger's "one and only place of refuge and withdrawal. Here amid bags and baskets, outer wraps and better garments saved for disembarking, towels and private drinking cups and teapots, each of us undressed for the night and dressed in the morning."

The compartments were filthy and foul-smelling. "Sweeping is the only form of cleaning done," the government report noted. "Sometimes the process is repeated several times a day. This is particularly true when the litter is the leavings of food sold to the passengers by the steward for his own profit. . . . No sick cans are furnished and not even large receptacles for waste. The vomitings of the seasick are often permitted to remain a long time before being removed."

The report continues: "No woman with the smallest degree of modesty, and with no other convenience than a washroom, used jointly with men, and a faucet of cold salt water, can keep clean amidst such surroundings for twelve days or more. . . . The toilets for women . . . baffle description. Each room or space was exceedingly narrow and short, and instead of a seat there was an open trough, in front of which was an iron step and back of it a sheet of iron slanting forward. On either side wall was an iron handle. The toilet was filthy."

After enduring twelve crossings in ships similar to the *Stampalia*, the Senate committee researchers concluded that congestion in steerage was "so intense, so injurious to health and morals that there is nothing on land to equal it. That people live in it only temporarily is no justification of its existence."

The shipping lines were unmoved. "The common plea," the Senate report pointed out, "is that better accommodations cannot be maintained because they would be beyond the appreciation of the emigrant and because they would leave too small a margin of profit." It is a familiar tune, the anthem of exploitation, and as I leafed through the dreary report I thought of the unfeeling papers in Phyllis's Social Security dossier and of the callous notice from the Times Square Motor Hotel. Perhaps steerage was an apt introduction to the American institutions that would orchestrate her final years.

Santa Maria Capua Vetere sits just above the ankle on the narrow shinbone of Italy, just north of Naples in the province of Campania, in the region known as the *Mezzogiorno*. It is now, as it was when Michele Iannotta left it, one of the poorest regions of a country that has many poor regions. The Italians refer to the *Mezzogiorno* in many ways. One of them is "the land that time forgot."

The life of a peasant family in the *Mezzogiorno* was hard, and America loomed like a fabled continent with the promise, if not of riches, certainly of more comfort and the chance to get ahead. Michele Iannotta was one of more than 3 million *contadini*—peasant farmers—who left the *Mezzogiorno* for America in the first fifteen years of the new century.

Once, Santa Maria Capua Vetere had been great. The Etruscans built a walled City of Seven Gates there and filled it with temples, amphitheaters, and two huge forums. It was a rich city with fertile farms and large-scale factories that produced the finest bronze and iron works in Italy. In time it became the terminus of the first leg of the Appian Way from Rome.

The Romans had added more temples to the city and built a famous school for gladiators there.

During the Punic Wars, the city aligned itself with Hannibal, who wintered there in 216 B.C., enjoying what the great Roman historian Livy called the "leisure of Capua" while he waited to resupply his army for an attack on Rome. Rome so severely punished Capua for helping Hannibal that for two centuries it failed to recover and Cicero spoke of it as the "abode of the politically dead." Caesar ultimately restored it with thousands of new colonists and by Trajan's time in the first century, it was prospering again.

But these glories had crumbled into dust centuries before Michele Iannotta came into the world. Nothing remained of the temples and amphitheaters and the school for gladiators but a few outcroppings of chiseled stone for a boy to climb on.

Michele Iannotta tilled the rocky soil with a hoe. The land had long ago been worked to death, and farming must have seemed futile. He had reason to know that there was more to be had from the world than could be scratched from the tired earth of Santa Maria Capua Vetere. For, as Popeye had told me, he had been in the Italian army and that insured that he would have seen something of the outside world; Naples was only thirty miles distant, but a world away to most of the peasants of Santa Maria Capua Vetere, whose only means of transportation was their feet or perhaps a donkey.

Certainly there was little to keep Michele Iannotta, and restless men like him, in worn-out towns such as Santa Maria Capua Vetere. Every day hundreds of poor, dissatisfied men yearning for a better life left from the ports of Italy bound for America.

They were, as an American public health doctor in Naples put it: "ignorant but with splendid adaptability, quick to learn, bright considering that he is a descendant of a race ill treated for centuries. . . . They are rugged and strong . . . and possess great endurance."

These sturdy peasants of the *Mezzogiorno* left their homeland not for political or religious freedom but for *pane e lavoro*—for bread and work. They left in such numbers that emigration became a major Italian industry, supporting more than 10,000 people—ticket agents, stevedores, recruitment agents, dockside hucksters, draymen, merchant seamen, ship suppliers, government agents, and port officials.

The immigrants arrived at Ellis Island, many of them with tags on their clothing indicating their destinations so agents of their new employers could steer them to their jobs in the vineyards of Southern California, the mines of Pueblo, Colorado, the mills of Pittsburgh, the goldfields of the Yukon. But most remained in New York, where they dug their livings from the earth with "peek and shuvil" or, like Michele Iannotta, scrounged out meager livings from what others discarded: rags, broken bottles, bones, scrap metal.

Whatever their illusions when they stepped off the boat, they would soon learn that in *La Mecca Dollaro* the streets not only weren't paved with gold, many weren't paved at all—and they were expected to pave them, at wages lower than those paid to almost anyone else. A daily wage schedule for workmen building the Croton Reservoir, New York City's upstate water supply, in 1898 shows how the transplanted *contadini* were regarded:

> Common labor, white—$1.30 to $1.50
> Common labor, colored—$1.25 to $1.40
> Common labor, Italian—$1.15 to $1.25

By the time Michele Iannotta arrived in New York, the wages for Italian laborers had gone up, perhaps to a princely $1.50 a day. But, surviving from day to day on the barest necessities, the transplanted *contadini* lived by the maxim that, as turn-of-the-century journalist-reformer Jacob Riis wrote: "It is not what one makes but what he saves that makes him rich."

Somehow, Riis marveled, the "greenhorn" Italian managed "to turn the very dirt of the streets into a hoard of gold, with which he either returns to his Southern home, or brings over his family to join in his work and in his fortunes. . . ."

No more than a year after he arrived here, Michele Iannotta managed to convert his "hoard of gold"—about $40, the earnings of a month—into a steamship ticket for his wife and infant daughter.

They arrived on May 19, 1915. The old New York *Trib-une* reported that the air that day was hot and motionless.

Photographer Lewis Hine's eloquent images of arriving immigrants, taken in a burst of flame with a five-by-seven flashpan camera and preserved in the collection of the New York Public Library, put me there:

Hundreds of men, women, and children are crowded on the top decks of the ship, bags in hand, waiting to step down the gangplank to the Ellis Island ferry that will take them to the vast complex, turreted like a Byzantine fairy-tale castle. There they undergo medical exams and are quizzed on their political beliefs; disease carriers, criminals, and anarchists are sent back.

The photographs are rich with the moment: a family waiting for its luggage, a mother embracing her child, a woman, her face lined with fatigue, resting against her bundles on a bench. I can almost hear the roar of voices, the tread of feet, the tears of children confused and afraid.

There is one photograph in particular: A young mother, her head bare, cradles her infant child in one arm. With the other hand she struggles to maintain her grip on the heavy burlap sack that contains their clothing and the few possessions they could bring with them to begin their new life *oltre mare*, beyond the sea.

I see in my mind's eye little Filomena carried by her mother, who, filled with anticipation and anxiety, waits to learn if she will survive the inquisition at *Isola della Lacrima*, the Isle of Tears, and be allowed to join her husband in the house on Connover Street in the section of Brooklyn called Red Hook. It strikes me that, sixty-seven years later, Phyllis Iannotta would die on the streets of New York as she had come to them—with everything she owned stuffed into a sack.

The trip to Red Hook, made by boat across the East River in those days, takes only a few minutes by car now through the Brooklyn-Battery Tunnel. But now, as then, Red Hook is not a place people rush to see. It has always been Brooklyn's poor relation, an isolated peninsula linked more closely, it sometimes seems, to far-off ports than to the rest of New York City. The tunnel to Manhattan, whose stately skyline lords over tiny Red Hook, wasn't completed until 1950 and there still is no subway stop there.

Washed by the Atlantic, Red Hook juts out into New York Harbor, bristling with docks and piers, great symbols of the power and wealth of America, and falls literally in the shadow of the Statue of Liberty, the great welcomer of immigrants.

Since the Dutch came three centuries before, Red Hook has been a home to immigrants brought by the ships of a hundred ports: Germans, Swedes, Norwegians, Irish, Welsh, Italians; seafarers and dockworkers, laborers and factorymen, the skilled and the unskilled, communicating in the dialects of half a dozen nations, jammed together cheek by jowl, struggling, not always in harmony, for their piece of the American pie.

Today, Red Hook is a study in decay: burned-out buildings, vacant lots, litter-strewn streets. About 12,000 people are squeezed into this half-mile-square neck of land, nearly 50 percent of them Hispanic, about 25 percent black, nearly all of them poor: the median income in Red Hook is about $9,000 a year; roughly 25 percent of its inhabitants are on welfare. The per-capita crime rate is one of the highest in the borough.

In the midst of all this, Public School 15 provides, if not a beacon, at least a ray of hope for the future. Here in a modern, low-slung building, as clean and bright as any school in the city, there is a sense of pride everywhere—in the colorful melange of student artwork on the walls, in the faces of the children and their teachers, even in the bird feeder that principal George Morfessi keeps well stocked to show his pupils that the joys of nature can be felt even in Red Hook.

"We're very proud of our school," Morfessi said as he led me down a long flight of stairs to the basement storage room, past box after box of books and paste and crayons and chalk and rulers. "Of course, this is a new school—the one your Miss Iannotta attended would have been P.S. 30, that was closed years and years ago. We took over all their records, kept them all these years."

He pointed to a row of shelves packed floor to ceiling with dust-covered cardboard boxes. "Here they are," he said. "They go back to the turn of the century. I can't vouch for what you'll find, but if she did go to P.S. 30 the records you're looking for ought to be here. Take all the time you need."

I popped open one of the sealed cartons, and a cloud of dust and bits of ancient paper billowed out into my face. Inside were stacks of class books dating back to the 1890s.

Here, with any luck, I would find not only Phyllis's school records but those of her classmates—people who might still be tracked down, who might remember playing with her on Connover Street, or swimming with her in the murky waters of the Atlantic Basin only a few blocks from the school, or perhaps carving her initials into a tree on Sullivan Street outside the house that Popeye remembered in his drunken ramblings.

Hour after hour, through box after box, book after book, page after page, I searched for some record of Phyllis until all the names, written with pedagogical precision in brown ink, blurred together: Anderson, Constance; Bavosa, Anna; Bjelka, Francis; Cuccicio, Concetta; Jaffe, Gladys; Jannetto, Philomena; LaTorr, Louisa; Martella, Viola . . . It took a few seconds to penetrate. *Jannetto, Philomena.* The spelling had been Ellis Islandized, but the address and the birthdate left no doubt.

I'd found what I'd come for, or at least a fragment of it, in a yellowed and crumbling eight-by-ten-inch pupil-progress book for the first-grade students of Sarah J. Burns. It covered September 1920 to February 1921. Before the day was out, I'd find six more books. They weren't pupil report cards but teachers' class record books with only sketchy cumulative information. Still, they gave me a glimpse of the little girl I'd come to Red Hook to find.

Physically, she was stocky, 111 pounds at age twelve, and short, only four feet eleven inches in the seventh grade (but at that already two inches taller than her mother). From the third grade on she wore thick glasses to correct eyesight that deteriorated progressively to 20/100.

She was a reasonably bright kid, but no Goody Two-shoes. At year's end, her first-grade teacher, Sarah J. Burns, awarded her a B for her schoolwork but only a C in deportment. It was a pattern she'd follow for the next six years.

It was after five o'clock when I finally emerged from the basement with my treasure trove. George Morfessi and his entire staff, except for one lone janitor, were gone from the building, and I reluctantly left the class books on the principal's desk with a note: "I struck it rich. Will return first thing tomorrow to make copies. Many thanks."

Children were still coming to school when I returned to P.S. 15 the next morning. George Morfessi greeted me enthusiastically. "I've got someone I want you to meet," he told me. "She's my attendance clerk. Been here forever. Grew up in Red Hook, went to old P.S. 30 herself. We think of her as the unofficial neighborhood historian. She might be able to give you some insight." He flipped on the school public-address system. "Adele Ramsey. Adele Ramsey. Come to the office please. Thank you."

A few minutes later a sandy-haired middle-aged woman presented herself at the principal's desk. Morfessi introduced us and showed her the aging class books. She inspected them. "Interesting," she said. "Very interesting. I went to P.S. 30, you know, but many years after this, about ten years."

She opened one of the books and turned its fragile pages carefully. "Sarah Burns," she said, seeing the teacher's name. "Now there was a teacher." She ran her finger down the page. "Well, well. Look at this." She laughed. "I'll be . . . He always told me he did well in school." She pointed to the name on the page. "Edward Ramsey," she said. "That's my husband!"

She said she would arrange for me to meet him, but weeks passed before he would grant an interview. When we met he was cordial but not eager. It was clear he resented being pressed into service by his wife.

Wiry, with a sharply chiseled face and hair the color of tarnished pewter, Edward Ramsey sat in the kitchen of his neat little house on Coffey Street, only a few blocks from the tenement at 137 Connover Street where school records showed the Iannotta family had lived when Filomena started school. "I haven't got much time . . . ," he began. I flopped the class books on the kitchen table in front of him. "Take a look," I said. "This won't take long."

He opened one and leafed through it. His name was written in it, as it was in each of the books, in the fine Edwardian script of his teachers of more than half a century ago: Sarah J. Burns, Gertrude B. McMahon, Anna J. Foster, H. M. O'Hara. They had been Phyllis's teachers too, strict no-nonsense women who ruled their classrooms with firm hands, which they were not averse to cracking on the skulls of students who spoke too quickly or learned too slowly.

Ramsey ran a gnarled finger down the page of his first-grade class book. "Thomas O'Hara, Paul Albert, George Schoen . . . My God, I haven't thought of some of these people for fifty years." His eyes glistened with nostalgia. "You know how it is, we just sort of drifted apart as we grew up, I guess. Most of them moved away. Not too many stayed in Red Hook, like me . . . "

Like his father and his father's father, Ramsey had been born in Red Hook and had lived there all his life. "My God," he said, beginning the litany of old men everywhere, "how this neighborhood has changed. I should have got out years and years ago, but this," he said with a sweep of his hand meant to take in not only his house but all of Red Hook, "is my home, my roots. I'll probably die here when my time comes . . .

"Yes, I remember some of these kids. Sure. Grew up

76

with 'em. But this one of yours, I don't know." He stared into space. "Filomena Iannotta," he said. "Iannotta . . . Iannotta. I can't say for sure I remember the name. That's a long, long time ago."

He shook his head from side to side as if trying to shake loose the memories. He stared at the class book. "William Prendergast, him I remember. He became a New York detective. Retired now, I suppose. And Helen Petersen, I remember her for sure, and Norman Munsen, he was sort of heavyset." The old man began drumming his fingers on the tabletop. "Fil-o-mena I-an-not-ta," he said, accenting each syllable with a beat. "I don't know. I just don't know . . . "

Adele Ramsey placed a bottle of rye whiskey in front of us. She smiled. "Maybe this will help you remember," she said, pouring us each a generous shot. We downed the shots quickly and poured a second to sip.

Ramsey toyed with his glass. "Fil-o-mena I-an-not-ta." He muttered the name half to himself. "Did you say she wore glasses?" I hadn't said, but of course she had—thick glasses, the kind you'd remember even years later. Ramsey shut his eyes tightly. "I see this little girl with glasses and very dark hair," he said. "It's funny. I just see her standing there wearing a waddyacallit, a frock. It's like a picture, kind of dim." His voice trailed off. The image had faded.

"I don't know," he said. "Sometimes I think I remember her, then I don't." The old man looked disappointed that he couldn't remember more. But I was beginning to see young Filomena clearer than before.

Adele Ramsey broke the silence. "Look at this," she said, tapping a finger on Phyllis's pupil record card. "Your girl sure moved around a lot. Eight homes in as many years—

137 Connover, 118 Sullivan, 290 Van Brunt, then back to Connover just a few doors away from the first place. She's only there for a year and she moves again, across the street, then again over to 315 Van Brunt, then 80 Sullivan and back to Connover Street. That's like a lot of the kids we have over at the school. Poor people, they move around a lot."

Indeed they do, I thought. Poverty has a way of rousting people, uprooting them. Fires, rent increases, evictions all keep the poor in a constant state of forced migration: always on the move, never going anywhere.

"All those addresses," Ramsey mused. "They make her a Pointer, a Pointer from Hocken Valley." He explained: "See, here in Red Hook there are Pointers and Creekers. When I was a kid I was a Pointer. We were the ones living on the Point—the part that juts out into the Bay. The Creekers, they got their name from the creek that used to run into Erie Basin. That's all covered over now. The Creekers, they went to P.S. 27 over on Nelson Street."

The memory of it made him grin like a mischievous little boy. He hit his fist into the palm of his left hand. "They were the enemy, see, and we'd fight with them just about every day. Things got pretty rough—kids would wind up with bloody noses, sometimes get their teeth knocked out. But it was all man-to-man, just fists. No knives or guns like today." A retired steamfitter, Ramsey looked to me as if he could still take care of himself on the tough streets of Red Hook.

"I feel sorry for the kids growing up here now," he continued. "This neighborhood has changed so much I can hardly recognize it—all the abandoned buildings, these crazy junkies, kids with guns . . .This used to be a great place to be a kid. Why, we used to go swimming down between the barges at Edison Beach. Girls could come too, sometimes. But they weren't allowed down at the water by the old saw mill." He laughed. "We used to call that Bare Ass Beach, because we'd go in in our birthday suits. Yeah, we had a great time—fightin', swimmin', playin' games like kick the can, stickball, ringalevio, stuff like that. Kids today, they don't know what they're missing."

Adele interrupted. "Tell him about Hocken Valley," she said. He answered impatiently. "I'm getting to that. Just hold your horses." He finished his drink, poured himself another and offered me the bottle.

"Hocken Valley," he said. "That's where all the Italians lived. Called it that because if you had something to hock, that's where you'd go." He laughed. "There weren't any real pawn shops that I know of. It's just that everybody was always out in the streets, haggling, making deals. It was exciting. Strange foods, homemade wine—you could get a quart jar of dago red for twenty-five cents back then, maybe less—peddlers going from door to door. It was a very poor neighborhood, and everybody was working some angle or other. They *had* to hustle to make a go of it."

There is no "Italian section" in Red Hook anymore, and Hocken Valley is just a memory. The voices of Calabria, Sicily, and Naples have been replaced by the staccato dialects of San Juan, Havana, and Santo Domingo. But the building at 137 Connover Street still stands, or at least the shell of it does—vacant and gutted, its windows covered with sheets of tin and its door sealed with a wall of cinder blocks. All that remains to evoke Phyllis's time is the elaborate wrought-iron fire escape that still climbs four stories across the dirty, red-brick facade.

I tried to picture it as it was more than sixty years ago. Photos in the local history section of the Brooklyn Public Library framed my imagination: Little Filomena on the fire escape, surrounded by sheets and other laundry hanging from the grillwork; Carmella Iannotta inside leaning over a black cast-iron stove as kettles and cauldrons simmered on coal-fed burners.

I saw the room as small and crowded, the walls a dirty yellow and stained with age, the narrow tongue-and-groove floorboards worn gray, for this place had been at least twenty years old and had been the home to perhaps a dozen desperately poor families before the Iannottas had come to live there.

I added a spot of color: on the wall over the sagging iron-framed bed, a gaudy lithograph of Santa Lucia, the patron saint of the *Mezzogiorno*, whose picture was found in Italian homes all over America. In one hand the beautiful white-clad maiden carried a lantern to show she knew "the way"; in the other hand, a sword, symbol of her role as protectress. And at her feet, a platter bearing her own disembodied eyes, torn from her, legend has it, by the tyrant who martyred her.

(In Italian churches everywhere, communicants with sight problems would light candles at the statue of Santa Lucia and place little replica eyes at its feet. I thought of Phyllis's thick glasses and imagined her mother kneeling before the saint.)

As I entered the Iannotta home in imagination, Hocken Valley came to life outside the window: peddlers crying *"Roba dalla mia! Roba dalla mia!"*—"My own goods!"— hawked cabbages, live chickens, tin housewares, and suits of clothes from pushcarts or from boxes strapped across their shoulders; the hurdy-gurdy man ground out his tune for the pennies of the passersby; children played in the streets; men gathered to play cards in the *caffè* on the next block; and friends sat on the stoops, avoiding the heat of the tenements and talking about the old days on the other side.

The *pescheria* down the street sold fresh calamari, tasty scungilli, and a dozen varieties of fish brought in that day from the Atlantic, and at the *pizzicheria* around the corner the air was ripe with the spicy-sweet aroma of salami and cheeses hanging from the rafters.

These were the sights and sounds and smells of Red Hook when Phyllis was a girl, and they would remain the same year after year, pleasant for their dependability. But after September 27, 1918, Phyllis's first day at school, their comfort would be invaded with conflict.

For there she would learn for the first time that there was a different way to live. From the age of six, she would be caught in a tug-of-war between two cultures, *la via vecchia* and *la via nuova*, the old way and the new way, the Neapolitan way and the American way.

They would be painful lessons.

Anti-immigrant sentiment had reached fever pitch in America. By 1918, the "huddled masses" had become the "invading hordes," and politicans felt free to argue in the strongest terms for strict limitations on immigration. The new Italian-Americans, with their extroverted social life, their love of strange foods—snails, squid, conch—and their public displays of Roman Catholicism replete with processions, statues, and the trappings of superstition offended the staid Protestant majority. Beatings, lynchings, and house burnings in cities across the country had become increasingly common.

And why not? President Wilson himself had warned:

"Hyphenated Americans . . . have poured the poison of disloyalty into the arteries of our national life. Such creatures of passion, disloyalty and anarchy must be crushed out."

Little Filomena's teachers had their marching orders. With chalk and copybook and the stinging slap of rulers they fanned the fires under the melting pot. H. M. O'Hara, Anna J. Foster, Sarah Burns, Gertrude McMahon—these were the women whose mission it was to make Filomena Iannotta an American, to teach this Italian-speaking child to mouth the incomprehensible words of the Pledge of Allegiance, to break her of her peasant habits, and to remind her in ways subtle and not so subtle that the beliefs her parents held dear were inferior, small-minded, and even unpatriotic.

Most transplanted *contadini* viewed these teachers as *stranieri*, outsiders, as enemies of *l'ordine della famiglia*, the welfare of the family, the most important of all institutions, more sacred than church, state, or self.

In 1900, 70 percent of the inhabitants of the Campania, the region of the Iannottas' birth, were illiterate, and as Richard Gambino points out in his book *Blood of My Blood: The Dilemma of the Italian Americans*, most held to the "much-quoted *contadino* saying to the effect that only a fool makes his children different from himself. . . . The time spent learning to read could better be used in learning the precious lessons of manhood and womanhood and in working for the family's daily bread and its vital competitive position."

The Italians' antischool bias was so deeply ingrained that even as late as 1969 a U.S. Census Bureau study on the educational accomplishments of major ethnic groups showed that only 27.6 percent of the Italian-American respondents over age thirty-five had completed high school and fewer than 5.9 percent had completed four years of college, lower than all but Hispanic-Americans.

Certainly, Filomena's parents would have wanted their daughter to be *ben educata*. But to the immigrant Italian family that had nothing to do with schoolwork. Being "well educated" meant having the rigid rules of Italian family life woven into the fabric of one's being.

A young girl would be taught at home to know her place, to live by the codes that had guided her mother and her mother's mother and all the mothers of their family beyond memory. She would be taught *la serieta*, the art of womanliness, at her mother's knee. She would be taught to cook and to sew and, of course, to keep an immaculate home. She would be counseled on how to walk and talk and dress, and on the subtleties of haggling at the market.

These were the things a woman needed to know, and they could not be learned from books. Her home was her school. It was a finishing school, but it had nothing to do with the white-gloved, tea-pouring femininity taught in American finishing schools. It was a school of the real world, where girls learned to be *scaltra*—clever and practical.

A 1914 *Century* magazine article lamented that, of all the immigrants, Italians had "the lowest proportion of children in school, and the highest proportion of children at work."

Phyllis's school records, like those of many of her Italian classmates, indicate that she was frequently absent from school. There is nothing in her school health records to indicate serious illness, so perhaps, like many Italian children of the period, she was taken out of school to work beside her mother, helping with the piecework Italian families did to make ends meet: sewing buttons on cards, making artificial flowers, putting labels on milk bottles.

Phyllis was eight years old when her brother was born into the strong hands of a midwife on the bed in the front room of the Iannottas' cramped flat at 118 Sullivan Street in Red Hook. The birth of a son, bearer of the family name, was the cause of great celebration in even the poorest Italian homes. Friends and neighbors would have knocked on the Iannotta door to express their congratulations, to glimpse the new hope of the Iannotta family, and to drink a glass of the red wine, possibly made by a *compare*, a special friend, in anticipation of the event.

It fell upon Phyllis to care for her little brother, to change his diapers, to rock him when he cried. "She was like a mother to me," Popeye told me one night over boilermakers at Kilroy's. "She took care of me when I was little. One thing I remember is when I was a little kid, my father, he was a junk man, he found this old wagon, you know a kid's wagon, and he fixed it up and painted it red and my sister she used to take me for rides in it."

Life for the junkman's family could not have been easy. "We was poor, real poor," Popeye told me. "We didn't have much. They was good, hardworkin', honest people, my mom and dad. But they didn't do too good."

The Iannottas' poverty is reflected in a school nurse's note that Phyllis suffered from nutitional problems when she was in third grade. That was in 1922, the year of Philip's birth. Had she gone hungry so he could eat? If so, it would have been the first of a lifetime of sacrifices she would make for him. "My sister," Popeye would tell me again and again. "She always stuck up for me. We'd fight back to back."

In 1929, when Phyllis was fifteen, her family moved to Brooklyn's Sunset Park, another waterfront neighborhood not far away, putting the comfortable familiarity of Hocken Valley behind them. Now they lived in a world of blond-haired, blue-eyed Swedes, Norwegians, and Finns, many of whom worked at nearby Bush Terminal, the largest deep-water industrial port in the world.

Here raw materials were unloaded from the ships of twenty-five steamship lines, converted into finished goods in on-site factories, stored in block after block of warehouses, or loaded onto the freight cars of its own railway system and shipped to outlets across the country.

I never learned why Michele Iannotta left Red Hook. The stolid blond-haired, blue-eyed residents of the area did not share his life-style: there were no Italian cafés where he could drink red wine and play *scopa*, the card game of the *Mezzogiorno;* there were no boccie courts; there was not even a good Italian market.

Nor did his neighbors share his poverty.

Then, as now, the people of Sunset Park enjoyed a higher standard of living than those of Red Hook, and it is difficult to know if the Iannottas managed to improve their lot by the move or if they merely suffered the difficulties of being poor among the more well-to-do.

Occasionally, Popeye recalled, his father found work on the docks, but times were hard, jobs were scarce, and mostly Michele Iannotta continued to eke out a meager living pushing his cart through the streets in search of rags and scrap metal he could resell for a few pennies a pound.

The family lived in a house at 254 42nd Street, only a few blocks from the terminal. It was torn down years ago to make way for the garages, warehouses, and small factories that now dominate the area. But in the local history section of the Brooklyn Public Library there is a photo of a house that stood only a block away. It is a shabby, two-story clapboard house in a long row of shabby, two-story clapboard houses on a desolate street overshadowed by Bush Terminal. There is little reason to believe that the Iannotta home was much different.

Only five blocks away on a bluff overlooking the harbor, surrounding the park that gives the section its name, the brownstones of the bluebloods of Sunset Park stand in stark contrast to the clapboard houses of the wharf district. It is clear that, however they may have benefited from the move, the Iannottas traded life in one slum for life in another, and that the proximity of their rich neighbors must have served as constant reminder to Phyllis of her standing on the social ladder of Brooklyn.

"Oh, yeah," Popeye remembers, "they called us guinea and wop and meatball. Every day it was like that. That's why we was in so many fights."

Phyllis was a seventh grader when they moved from Red Hook, and she enrolled in Dewey Junior High, a dignified red-brick school an easy walk from her home. There, for the first time, she had classmates who came from all over Brooklyn. There, girls in nice dresses walked home to town houses with sparkling chandeliers framed in lace-curtained windows while she returned to a two-story white-washed box. If Phyllis had her problems at P.S. 30, she was more of a misfit here. She was thirteen, the junkman's daughter, and a "wop."

Perhaps it was at Dewey Junior High, in a bid for acceptance, that she surrendered her soft Neapolitan accent for the hard-edged nasality of Brooklyn English. Perhaps it was there that Filomena became Phyllis. But Phyllis could not surrender her past so easily. Every day after the final bell at three o'clock, she would have to go home. And there she remained Filomena.

If the Iannotta family was like many of the Italian families of Brooklyn, Filomena was discouraged from mixing with *stranieri*. If some of her classmates were to ask her to join them at the soda fountain on 49th Street, she would have been expected to say no. If a young man suggested she go with him to Sunset Park to watch the ships from the promontory overlooking the harbor, she would have been expected to decline.

Venite subito a casa dopo la scuola—come home right after school—would have been a family byword, a guarantee against *i costumi Americani*, the permissive American ways.

Whether Phyllis suffered under these restrictions is only guesswork. I searched long and hard, even put ads in local newspapers, but I was unable to locate a single schoolfriend who could remember the short, dark-haired teenager with thick glasses. But this much I do know: Phyllis never completely abandoned *la via vecchia* for *la via nuova*, and many years later people who did not know her name would describe her to me as "that old Italian woman."

The conflict between the two ways of life apparently took its toll. Phyllis was at Dewey only a few months when her grades plunged from Bs to near failing in every subject—notably including deportment.

Finally on March 6, 1930, Warren Van Name, the dour and distinguished principal of Dewey Junior High School, granted her an employment certificate allowing her to drop out and seek work. The document was conveyed without pomp, and the circumstances were less than auspicious. But to Phyllis's parents, the flimsy slip of paper must have been more valuable than any diploma. At last their daughter was going to get a job. She was going to help support *la famiglia*.

Phyllis was not yet yet sixteen, and the nation was in the throes of the Great Depression.

Flesh
and
Blood

Philip was eight when Phyllis quit school to go to work, and already, his school records show, he had earned a reputation as a troublemaker and a truant. He failed second grade twice. On his report card, after the words "Not Proficient In," his teacher had written with cruel veracity: "Anything."

By the time he was ten, Philip was so incorrigible he was sent to Mount Loretto, a Catholic reformatory on the shores of Raritan Bay on Staten Island, where optimistic priests believed they could reverse his life with fresh air, good food, and religious training.

But Philip wasn't buying it.

"I run away from there," he boasted at one of our meetings at Kilroy's. "Didn't like it, so why stay? Not for me. Simple as that." Somehow, this streetwise Brooklyn boy managed to find his way across bucolic Staten Island to a ferry slip almost twenty miles away and stow away aboard a boat that took him to the docks of Brooklyn at 39th Street, only a few blocks from his home.

"My sister, she found me sittin' on a stoop not far from where we was livin'," he recalled. "She was mad as hell, but took me home and treated me right, and when the man came lookin' for me she told me right away so I could jump out the window and run."

Phyllis covered up for Philip that day, as she would every time he asked her to. He was her brother. She had to stick up for him. It was part of the code by which they were raised: *nostru sangu per il nostru sangu*, blood for our blood. But the incident frightened her, and, just as she would go to Father Rappleyea nearly sixty years later, she turned then to Father O'Mara at St. Rosalie's Church in Sunset Park.

The old priest spoke to the boy and decided what he needed was a little discipline. He would make him a St. Rosalie's Cadet. Philip would receive quasi-military training, get to wear a snappy uniform, and march in all the parades.

"We had white pants, see, and these big hats with feathers in 'em," Philip recalls. "It was nice, real nice." And, he remembers, "When I told Father O'Mara I didn't have no money to buy no white pants, you know what he done? He bought 'em himself outa his own pocket. He was one swell guy."

But the good influence of Father O'Mara didn't last long. Philip bounced in and out of reform schools in the city and upstate New York throughout his childhood, while his sister worked to support the family.

90

There are no records of what the jobs were that Phyllis had quit school to take. They were before Social Security came into being. But she could not have won much freedom from them. She would still have been expected home every day after work, still expected to turn her earnings over to her mother, still expected to care for Philip when he wasn't "away."

During the war she worked in a defense plant at the Brooklyn Navy Yard. Defense Department files show that in 1944 she was a $6.16-a-day electrician's helper wrapping magnetos and soldering connections on an assembly line. She was thirty then, and it is the first job she had for which a record exists.

The same records led me to Catherine Finstad (she was Catherine Hanak then), an animated sixty-year-old blonde housewife who had worked in the same plant with Phyllis and remained her friend for more than thirty-five years.

Finstad, now a grandmother, agreed to talk to me at her home, a simply furnished but cheery brownstone in Sunset Park. She had learned of Phyllis's death from my story in the *Daily News*. "My family tried to keep it from me," she told me. "They knew it would upset me. But they left the article out by mistake a few days later, and I saw it anyway. It *did* upset me. Phyllis was my son's godmother and we were very close. She said to me one time, 'You are like a mother and a sister and a friend all in one.'

"We got to know each other in the cafeteria at the Navy Yard during our breaks," Finstad told me. "Phyllis worked in the electrical shop; I was in the paint shop painting parts for ships. She would smile and say hello, and I'd smile back, but I really didn't want to get involved. I just wanted to get my candy bar and get back to work. Then one day, she sat down next to me and said, 'I'm going to make you my friend, whether you like it or not.' That was the beginning and we remained friends ever since."

Finally. After months and months of searching through school records, phone books, property records; after knocking on doors in neighborhoods where I knew she had lived; after placing ads in newspapers; after making an appeal on a local radio station—finally I had found someone who had actually known Phyllis Iannotta.

Catherine Finstad would put flesh on the pale skeleton I had assembled from dull and dusty pieces of paper. Slowly, Phyllis was coming to life—and she was full of life.

"Oh she was great fun, a real friend and wonderful company," Finstad told me. "She loved the Navy Yard. We all did, I guess. You know, the war was on and we were proud to be doing our part." She laughed. "We worked like hell during the week, but after work on Fridays, we'd take our paychecks to the bar around the corner and get a pitcher of beer and unwind. Somebody'd put a nickel in the juke box and before long some of the fellas we worked with would come over and start to talk. Phyllis was very outgoing and very direct. If she liked you she'd tell you straight out. Men liked that."

Invariably, one of them would wind up in a booth alone with Phyllis. Finstad smiled and shook her head. "No, she wasn't pretty. She wore glasses and was a little on the chunky side. God only knows why she wasn't skinny. She ate like a bird. But she was big from the waist down. She didn't exactly have what you'd call style, either—if skirts were long that year, she'd wear them short, or she'd mismatch the colors. She didn't seem to care much about that sort of thing."

But men didn't seem to notice: "Phyllis wasn't *un*attractive, either, and she was a marvelous listener. She had a quality that made people feel at ease; you could bare your soul to her. She was somebody a man could talk to."

Occasionally, a soldier or a sailor or one of the men from the assembly line would ask Phyllis out, and occasionally—although she could have been suspended for fraternizing with military men—she would go to the movies, a quiet dinner out at a modest neighborhood restaurant, or maybe a dance. Phyllis loved to dance. Jitterbug, the lindy, the Big Apple. She knew all the latest steps, and as Finstad described her movements, she evoked a sensuality the records I'd been poring over could never have revealed. When Phyllis danced the fox-trot, Finstad added, men remembered it—somehow she no longer seemed so plain.

"Sure, Phyllis went out on dates," her friend said. "But there was never anybody special, no romances or anything." She sighed. "It was sort of sad. Phyllis was like the classic old maid daughter. She stayed home and took care of her mother and father."

After less than a year at the Navy Yard, Phyllis had been promoted twice and was receiving $8.08 a day—enough to pull her family out of the slums of Sunset Park. They moved to a three-room flat in Bensonhurst, Brooklyn.

There is not much that can be said for Bensonhurst of the 1940s. "Undistinguished" is the word the 1939 *WPA Guide to New York* chose. At least it wasn't on the docks, and that was a move up for the Iannotta family. Yet in some ways, they might as well still have been in Santa Maria Capua Vetere. "They were a real Italian family," Finstad remembered. "They were very old-fashioned. Their house was always a pleasant, hospitable place and I was always welcome. But there wasn't anything American about them."

Phyllis's mother, by then old and fat, would waddle around the kitchen, preparing delicious meals, exotic to Catherine Finstad's American palate, of veal *alla parmigiana* or of pasta served with seafood in a rich, pungent tomato sauce.

But Carmella Iannotta was often sick, and she spent most days sitting in an armchair in the living room, surrounded by bottles of medicine. "Phyllis was forever running to the drugstore for medicine or carting her mother off to the doctor. It was very demanding."

Phyllis's father, as Finstad remembered him, was a "nice old man with a twinkle in his eye." He spoke practically no English, but "he would sit in the living room smoking his corncob pipe and listen to us talk. He would laugh at our jokes as if he understood them." But he, too, was old before his time and bent with years of hard labor.

"He would go out with the pushcart sometimes," Finstad said, "but I don't think that ever amounted to much." It was, in fact, a pathetic gesture: the age of the pushcart was long over; Michele Iannotta had become a relic.

The family's dependency on Phyllis, hinted at earlier by the frequency with which she was needed to help out at home, was now chronic. Phyllis ran the household.

"They were very poor," Finstad said. "They didn't have any nice things in the apartment. It was . . . I guess you would have to say shabby. They didn't have a bedroom suite or anything. No couch even. Just these old-fashioned hard-backed wooden chairs. But you'd never hear Phyllis complain. She was supporting the family, caring for her mother and father and doing everything. And they sometimes treated her as if she were a kid. I'd say to her, 'I don't know how you do it.' But she'd just laugh and say, 'What else can I do? They're my parents.' "

94

So Phyllis shopped and cooked and cleaned and sewed and did the laundry and haggled with bill collectors and fought with the landlord for more heat. And she kept a respectful silence when her parents continued to treat her as a child.

"They didn't give her much room for a life of her own," Finstad remembered. Even after Phyllis passed thirty and was in danger of becoming an old maid, "they were very strict with her, particularly when it came to the subject of men." Finstad's voice revealed traces of bitterness. "It was a shame. She sacrificed herself for them. Phyllis would have made a wonderful wife and mother. She was the godmother to my son Johnny, and she was terrific with him. She had patience and understanding. She loved kids and they loved her. But marriage? That just wasn't in the cards. She sacrificed herself for her family."

Another kind of testimony attests to Phyllis's steadfast devotion to her family: Philip's prison record and the years of correspondence she conducted with wardens in his behalf.

At sixteen, Philip was found guilty of shoplifting. He received a suspended sentence. Three years later, he was convicted of breaking into a candy store. The record does not show what he stole, and Popeye was reluctant, or unable, to provide details. "It was petty stuff," he insisted, "junk, just junk. Nothin' big. Nothin' to brag about." Still, he was put behind bars for five years in the state penitentiary at Elmira, a grim, gray-brick prison for first-offense felons.

Phyllis was then twenty-seven years old.

Her brother's rap sheet shows that by that time he had adopted the name Philip Gennaro. Perhaps he was protecting his family. Perhaps they did not want him to disgrace the family name by using it behind bars. Who knows? Perhaps Philip himself, his mind fried by booze, had long since forgotten the true reason by the time I met him. Perhaps it was a secret he did not care to reveal.

In any case, the name Iannotta appears nowhere in the records of the New York State Department of Corrections, and when Phyllis came to visit her brother, she always signed her name in the visitors' register as Fay Gennaro.

Prison records are not public record, but a state corrections official told me this much:

Phyllis visited often, and more often still she wrote impassioned letters to the warden begging him to release her brother, promising that she would see to it that he made something of his life. She had gotten a local junk dealer—perhaps a friend of her father—to write saying he would give Philip a job. But the warden was not impressed.

After less than a year at Elmira, Philip was transferred to the Napanoch State Institution for Male Defective Delinquents. Tests had determined he had a mental age of ten and an IQ of only 68. At Napanoch, inmates worked in shops making metal signs, wooden handles, and materials for shoes. Philip showed himself to be a "very poor worker," according to prison records. But he was handy with crafts and he had a "good ear for music."

So, while other young men hearkened to the call of the trumpet in places like Anzio and Iwo Jima, Philip played the bugle in the prison marching band.

After the war, with Philip still in prison, Phyllis continued to work in electronics, assembling radios and phonographs at firms in Brooklyn and Manhattan. At night, her Social

Security dossier shows, she moonlighted as a waitress and a kitchen helper, as a salesgirl in a jewelry store and a worker in a chewing-gum factory, even as a cleaning lady.

Her Social Security records also show that she never made much money. But she worked regularly and, judging by large gaps in reported earnings some years, frequently off the books. And so it went year after year: long hours at low pay in monotonous jobs, often day and night, to support Mama and Papa and the weary flat in Bensonhurst.

Years later she would tell her doctor that she would have liked to have married but that she had to take care of her parents instead. In fact, she told him, she remained a virgin until her father died. She was then thirty-five years old.

Michele and Carmella Iannotta died within months of each other, both of cancer in 1949. Phyllis "left work and then went right to the hospital," Finstad remembered, "first to see her dad, then to her mom. They were in different hospitals; her dad went in first and she never told him about her mother. He would complain and want to know why she wasn't spending more time with him. But she never told him the real reason. She was afraid it would kill him. It nearly killed *her* with all that running from one hospital to the other.

"She suffered the tortures of the damned when they were dying," Finstad recalled. "It was awful, just awful. They were very close. It hurt her very much to lose them, but she just kept it all inside. That was her way."

When her brother came home from prison for the funerals, he had her shoulder to cry on. But Phyllis never had anybody's shoulder to cry on. "She was like the Rock of Gibraltar," Finstad remembered. "But I know now that on the inside she was crying out."

Phyllis continued to live in her parents' home after they died, but the apartment was full of memories and of the constraints that went with them. Finstad remembered: "I used to tell her, 'Phyllis, it's time to go out on your own.' But she just had a hard time getting started I guess."

Her parents had been dead nearly four years when Phyllis finally showed her old friend an ad in the weekly *Home Reporter*: "1 rm. pvt. house, Bay Ridge. Furnished. For resp. single woman. $12 @ week in advance." Phyllis had circled it in red. "This could be it," she said. "This could be it."

First Love,
Lost Love

The shingle-covered house at 320 76th Street sits in the middle of a quiet block lined with oak and maple and sycamore. The sidewalks surrounding it are as clean and orderly as any in Dubuque, and there is a checkerboard symmetry about the entire neighborhood that seems out of place in Brooklyn.

The neat, narrow row houses with their tiny front yards and freshly painted fences exude an air of working-class stability. This is Bay Ridge, a neighborhood of families— of husbands who work with their hands, of wives who stay home to cook and clean, of children who go to school and dream of getting married and having kids and landing union jobs with good retirement benefits: factory workers, government workers, firemen, sanitationmen, cops.

It was a police officer, in fact, who answered Phyllis's

knock on a cold, gray November afternoon in 1955. Bob Hansen was working the day beat in the Boro Park precinct back then, and the money he got from renting the two rooms on the second floor of the old house at 320 76th Street was an important source of income.

Hansen is retired now. He spoke to me from a bed in his living room, where he has been confined since 1970, when he suffered a stroke.

"We had five kids," he told me, "starting with Richard, who was, what, about ten or eleven back then. Then there was the girls, Janice, Susan, and Audrey, and then the baby, Ken. He wasn't quite four months old then, I guess. That's a lot of mouths to feed on a cop's salary, so I worked a second job as a building engineer and we made two apartments on the second floor so's we could get the rent.

"The Russells—he worked on the docks, his missus she was pregnant at the time—rented the big one and Phyllis, she took the smaller one. She had to share the bath. We were glad to see her. We needed the money."

Hansen remembered that Phyllis arrived wearing a new dark cloth coat, a new dress, and a look of determination. He judged her with a cop's critical eye. "She looked straight at you when she talked," he recalled. "I liked that." He rented her the room.

"Phyllis was like a member of the family," his wife Evelyn told me as she made a pot of coffee in her neat Formica kitchen. She was a plain, gray-haired woman who wore a pressed apron to protect her pullover blouse and brown polyester slacks. She was what she appeared to be, a simple Brooklyn housewife. "We were shocked, absolutely shocked when we read she was murdered. She was so alive when she came here, so vivacious. She was very brainy, too. Always reading and doing crossword puzzles and such like.

The brainy ones, they're the ones that always crack first."

She paused. "You knew she had a nervous breakdown while she was living here?" She asked it as if she expected me to know.

I shook my head.

"Oh," she said. "She just fell apart . . . " Her voice trailed off. I waited for an explanation.

"Phyllis came here some time after her mother died," she began. "I think she'd been dead for several years, but Phyllis was still kind of broken up about it. Anyway, she was trying to start a new life for herself. So she put her things in storage and she moved from wherever it was she had been living.

"The room upstairs," she said, nodding in the direction of a long, narrow flight of stairs, "was furnished. Nothing fancy, understand, but enough for a woman alone." It was a simple room, Evelyn Hansen said, just a studio couch that doubled as a bed, a chair, a small table, a chest of drawers, a hot plate. But Phyllis saw the bright side. "It won't take much time to clean," she told her new landlord. For the next ten years, 320 76th Street would be Phyllis's home.

In time, Phyllis added lace curtains to the windows and put chintz slipcovers on the couch and the chair. She bought a rug for the floor and a lamp with a fringed shade to go next to the couch. On the walls she hung pink molded plaster ballerinas, a portrait of Christ at the Last Supper painted on velvet, and calendar pictures of various saints.

"Oh, those were good times, those times with Phyllis," Mrs. Hansen said nostalgically. "At least until the end . . . " She stared silently into her coffee.

"You told me she had a nervous breakdown," I tried. "What was that all about?"

"That was years after she came here. Maybe seven or

eight years. No, for all those years, Phyllis was very . . . "
She searched for the word. "I don't know. I guess you could
say regular. She was just regular."

Evelyn Hansen painted Phyllis as an ordinary woman
living an ordinary life in an ordinary house surrounded by
ordinary people, a life as predictable as the streets of Bay
Ridge. By then Phyllis was a full-time employee of Esquire
Radio, only a few blocks from home. Every day it was the
same: up at seven, work all day on the assembly line, home
by six-thirty for a quick supper cooked on her hot plate,
then maybe television or a game of cards with the Hansens,
and off to bed with a book or her crossword puzzle.

"Phyllis did love her crossword puzzles," she said. "You'd
always see her with one, chewing on a pencil and trying to
figure out what words to put in. And she was always reading
a book. Why, she'd read everything . . . I couldn't tell you
which ones exactly, I'm not much for reading myself, but
they were thick ones. Books about religion and history,
best-sellers, anything and everything."

To Evelyn Hansen, Phyllis seemed, "You know, sort
of—how should I put it?—intellectual, I guess." She said
the word with a touch of awe, as if Phyllis's interest in
books made her somehow superior. "Sometimes," she said,
"she and Bob would get to talking about politics, about what
the mayor was up to and such and I would just get left
behind." Then, concerned I might get the wrong impres-
sion, she quickly added: "She wasn't stuck up or anything
like that. It was just that she was real smart."

At first, Phyllis kept pretty much to herself. "It seemed
to us like she was shy," the landlady recalled. "She would
say hello, of course, and things like that. But she wasn't
outgoing. So one day I asked her if she would like to play

cards with us. I didn't think she'd say yes, but she was delighted. I guess she was a little lonely what with having no family to speak of and not many friends.

"Well, me and Mrs. Clancy (she's dead now, rest her soul) used to play cards every week, and Phyllis fit right in. We'd sit here at the kitchen table and talk and sew and play cards—brisk and 500 rummy mostly. I'm a pretty good cardplayer and Phyllis was good, too. We always had a good time."

Without asking, she got up and poured me another cup of coffee.

"Phyllis was always good to be with," she continued. "Sometimes on Saturday nights she and me and Bob would go over to the Olde Pumpe Inn on Third Avenue. They'd have this little Scandinavian band—you know, with an accordion?—and we'd dance the night away. We'd party into the wee hours, and come home all pooped. Phyllis would plop down in her chair, she always liked to sleep in a chair, don't know why but she did. Anyway, she'd catch a few hours sleep, then she'd get up and go to work fresh as a daisy. I don't know how she did it. And, oh, was she some dancer! Rumba, samba, you name it.

"Partners? No, she never had any trouble on that score. Men used to like dancing with her. She'd tell them she was ten years younger than she really was, and they'd believe it. She could get away with that." Phyllis would have been over forty by then.

"Did she date much?" I asked.

"I don't know about *much*, but sure, she'd see some fellas now and then. Nobody special. Except Kurt . . . "

"Kurt?"

"Yeah . . . " Her voice sank and she shook her head.

"Phyllis sure fell for him. He was a nice man. Kind of short and chunky, not exactly handsome or anything. But Phyllis really loved him. What a shame that turned out to be. A damn shame, if you'll pardon my language."

"They *were* a handsome couple, though," she said, and bit by bit Evelyn Hansen pieced together a description of Phyllis's first love. Kurt was about five feet eight and stocky with a barrel chest. He had short-cropped sandy hair, and he wore workman's clothes most of the time. His most distinguishing feature was his smile, which was broad and toothy. As Mrs. Hansen described him, he must have been engagingly boyish although she said she thought he was in his midthirties.

"He was jolly," she said. "Yes, I would definitely call him jolly. Always making jokes. Oh, how Phyllis loved him. She was crazy about him." She laughed. It was an embarrassed laugh. "Did I say crazy?" she said. "It was him that did it," she added bitterly. "He was the one that made her crazy. Him and that brother of hers."

Mrs. Hansen drew a deep breath and sighed loudly. She began to busy herself about the kitchen. It was clear she was dying to tell me all about Kurt. But she was not a gossip. Propriety required that I ask. And so I did.

She wiped her hands on her apron and sat down. "Well," she began, as if settling in for a long story, "I don't know if I should be telling you this . . . " She waited for a little encouragement. I gave it to her. "Well," she began again, "I really don't know where to begin." Before I could make some suggestions, however, she had launched her story.

"I don't know where they met, or how they got started. But he would come here every Saturday to see her. He always brought flowers or something. It was always a big deal for Phyllis. She'd spend the day cleaning and dusting and making things just so for him. Then she'd take a shower and fix her hair and put on perfume and get all dressed up in something nice . . . "

The love affair lasted two years. Every Saturday night Kurt appeared with his bouquet of flowers and his good-natured jokes about traveling salesmen and farmers' daughters and dogs who ordered drinks in bars. Everyone would laugh and feel good when he was there. And then he and Phyllis would go upstairs and the Hansens would wink knowingly.

"They didn't go out much," Mrs. Hansen said. "Maybe once in a while they'd go to a movie at the Alpine—Phyllis worked there for a while as a matron and I guess she got passes or something—and I think they took the train into the city to dance at Roseland a couple of times, and maybe they went to Coney Island in the summer. But mostly they just stayed up there in the room, don't you know, with the radio playing. Sometimes he'd bring a couple of steaks up and they'd cook them on the hot plate.

"Sometimes he stayed over. I knew about that, but we never talked about it. It was against our rules of course,"— she threw up her hands and shrugged—"But so what? What did I care, really? They seemed so happy."

But it was not that simple. For when Kurt tiptoed out of Phyllis's life on Sunday mornings, he tiptoed into another life—a life with a wife and children.

No one in the Hansen family ever knew Kurt's last name— Catherine Finstad would tell me later she never even learned his first name—or his occupation or where he lived. But, Evelyn Hansen said, "We knew he was married, because my daughter Janice, she was little then, picked up the extension phone when he was talking to Phyllis and she heard him say he couldn't see her. It was his daughter's birthday. Of course, we never said anything about it. They were grownups, after all."

If Phyllis brooded about this she kept it to herself. Her workaday life never wavered from its well-ordered path. At least on weekends she could allow herself the luxury of forgetting that she was forty-five years old and an old maid with virtually no hope of a husband to grow old with. Kurt was a bird in the hand, and he seemed to love her. She didn't complain.

And then, one day in September 1963, Philip Gennaro arrived on the Hansens' doorstep. He was a stranger to them. He had just been released from Auburn State Correctional Facility after doing two and a half years for receiving stolen property.

He wore an ill-fitting prison discharge suit. The too-long trousers hung comically on his bowed legs and his long arms protruded awkwardly from the sleeves of the jacket. His features were much like his sister's, but he wore his hair slicked into a pompadour, and he had the sullen, knowing look of someone who has spent most of his life behind bars. Janice Hansen, then a fifteen-year-old, remembered that his nose seemed to be stuck on his face, like the piece from a child's Mr. Potato Head.

Philip (no one in the Hansen household knew him as Popeye) was allowed to move rent-free into the upstairs room with his sister in exchange for occasional handyman chores. "He seemed nice enough," Evelyn Hansen remembered. "He was always coming and going. He didn't stay there every night. Phyllis talked about her brother all the time. But we didn't know he was an ex-con. That was the one thing she left out . . . "

Phyllis had told people her brother was "upstate" and had never mentioned his occupation. Occasionally, she would leave Brooklyn to visit him. Each visit was preceded by elaborate preparations: she would shop for presents—a sweater, perhaps, and, always, a carton of Lucky Strikes—and sometimes she would treat herself to a new dress, careful to make it pretty but proper. ("I always told her I liked her to look like a lady," Popeye told me one night. "I don't like it when a woman don't act like a lady.")

She would return the next day cheerful and bearing presents from him, crafts made in the prison workshops: ashtrays and plaques and, her favorite, an elaborate popsicle-stick church encrusted with bits of colored glass that found a permanent home on top of her large Emerson radio. The Hansens marveled at the craftsmanship and never suspected where it had been made, nor did they know of the long hours Phyllis spent alone in her room composing letters to prison wardens begging for her brother's release.

In the strict code in which she had been raised, such private pain—family pain—was not to be shared with outsiders, even if they were friends. But now Philip was home; they were a family again. Phyllis welcomed her brother into her new life, expecting that he would be glad for her newfound happiness.

Instead, he reacted with anger and animosity. "I don't think he and Kurt got along real well," Mrs. Hansen told me. "I think there were some problems there." In fact, Philip, intent on splitting them apart, inserted himself between Phyllis and her lover like a wedge.

"Yeah," Popeye told me one night over a meal in a Times Square fast-food joint, "I remember Fay was seein' some guy. Blond guy. I don't remember his name. Who cares? I didn't like him. First, he wasn't Italian, and second . . . " He shook his head as if to rid it of something. "I don't remember what the second thing was, but I remember I didn't like him. Told him so, too, more'n once.

"He called me a bum," Popeye said testily, spraying bits of chicken as he talked. "And I let him know what I thought about him. Nobody talks to me like that." Anger glared in his eyes. Even after all these years he still resented the "other man" in his sister's life. "I tol' the sonofabitch, I tol' him. Jesus, I tol' him . . . "

"What did you tell him?"

Popeye took another mouthful of chicken, wiped his mouth with his shirt sleeve, and got up. I would never get an answer to my question. But this much is safe to say, Philip still hadn't forgiven Kurt. Phyllis's lover had been an unforgivable intrusion, a threat.

Few people ever have to choose between the two best-loved people in their lives. On one hand, Phyllis's brother had been nothing but trouble to her from the moment he had loosed his first cry in the drab tenement in Red Hook. Kurt, at least, brought her flowers and made her laugh and had come to her bed on nights when she was lonely.

On the other hand, Philip was her brother. Her only family. She had fed him when he was a baby, washed him, clothed him, tucked him in at night. She had been like a mother to him. These things could not be forgotten.

All her life, Phyllis had always taken her brother's part— against the bullies of Red Hook, against sentencing judges, against prison wardens. Kurt had called her brother a bum.

They had argued, no doubt within Phyllis's hearing. It could not have enhanced her relationship with Kurt.

"Nobody was allowed to say a bad word about Philip, not when Phyllis was around," Evelyn Hansen said. "She was fiercely loyal to him. She loved him, very much."

One Saturday, Kurt simply did not come to the house on 76th Street with his bouquet of flowers and his jokes about farmers' daughters and traveling salesmen and dogs who ordered drinks in bars. And he never came again.

"I don't know what happened," Evelyn Hansen said. "He just stopped coming, just like that. No explanations. I don't think he phoned or wrote or anything. Who knows? Maybe his wife got wind of his little tête-à-têtes. Maybe it was Philip. Maybe he . . . just . . . got . . . bored." She accented each word individually as if just the memory of it filled her with anger.

"Of course, Phyllis never said a word about it. She was like that, you know. She could be starving and she'd never say she was hungry." She thumped her chest with the tips of her fingers. "Kept it all inside, don't you know. Kept it all inside, always. But oh, how it broke her spirit.

"She was never the same again, never. She stopped going out. Just stayed in her room most of the time. She left her job, stopped paying her rent, and just fell apart. And she never mentioned Kurt again."

The way Evelyn Hansen told it, in ten minutes over coffee, Phyllis's breakdown seemed to have happened in the span of only a few days. But in fact her deterioration took place over several years, culminating in the brief hospitalization I had discovered among her records.

The Monday after Kurt walked out of her life, Phyllis did not bother to go to work. She just stayed in her room waiting for word. Tuesday, Wednesday, Thursday, Friday: no word from Kurt. Saturday gave way to Sunday, and still no word. A week passed. A month. No Kurt.

Phyllis's world began to shrink. At first she went to work sporadically, then she stopped going altogether. She no longer came downstairs for the evening coffee klatches with Evelyn Hansen and her friend Mrs. Clancy. She no longer joined Bob and Evelyn for drinks and dancing at the Olde Pumpe Inn. She just sat for hours on end in the chair in her room.

"It was real tough on the kids," Evelyn Hansen said. "They loved her very much and she was terrific with them. They could always go up to her room and talk with her or play cards, or whatever. She was *there* for them in a way I couldn't be."

She explained: "You see, during this time I had to work nights to make ends meet, so I couldn't always be the perfect mother, if you know what I mean. Well, Phyllis was there to fill in the gaps, I guess you could say. She was like an aunt to them, especially to Richard. When he was a teenager, she was like his confidante, someone he could talk to, tell his problems to. Yeah . . ." She looked off wistfully. "Richard took what happened to Phyllis real hard."

Richard Hansen is now in his late thirties. He lives in Bay Ridge only a few blocks from his boyhood home and, like his father before him, is working at two jobs, struggling to support his wife and four kids. It is not easy, and the strain of it shows on his face. But when he spoke of Phyllis, his boyish features came alive and he looked more as he must have when Phyllis came to live at 320 76th Street.

He was a ninth grader then, fifteen years old, and by

his own admission a somewhat less than enthusiastic student. "Phyllis was real smart," he told me as his children played on the kitchen floor of his cramped apartment. "She was a good speller. I guess it was all those crossword puzzles she used to do. She sure did love her crosswords! Anyway, she really helped me get through school. Helped me get through life, I should say . . ."

He picked up his young son and hugged him for a moment, then put him down to play. His eyes were moist. He waved his hand across his face and shook his head as if to chase away his sadness. "What happened to Phyllis," he said, "well, that makes me feel real bad. She was very special to me."

He paused, collecting his thoughts. "What can I tell you? She was like a psychiatrist to me. You know, somebody you could talk to, tell anything to. She would listen. She would never laugh at you or make you feel like a stupid kid. You always had the feeling she really cared. You could tell her things and never worry that she'd blab. You know how important that is to a kid growing up?

"Take the time she caught me watching stag films in the basement . . ." A smile crossed his face and he chuckled. "See, one of my buddies got these, uh, blue movies and so we got hold of a projector and set it up downstairs at my place and we were watching them, you know, when along comes Phyllis. Boy, did she read us the riot act. She threw the guys out and then she came back and bawled me out real good. But you know, she never said a word to my parents. Not one word.

"Then there was the time I got drunk. I guess I was about sixteen. It was the first time I'd ever tied one on. I was *really* plastered, and I was walking down 76th Street like this . . ." He got up and staggered across the kitchen. "I somehow managed to get through the gate to the house, and I just passed out. I fell flat on my back and my feet kicked up in the air and hit the door." He slapped the table with his palm. "Bam! I was out like a light.

"Well, Phyllis was the only one home, and she heard the bang and came out to see what the hell was going on. She opened the door and there I was. At first she was scared, but when she saw I was drunk she got mad. Not real mad, but, like, I don't know, disappointed.

"She helped me up and gave me a little kiss and took me inside. She took me up to her room and pumped me full of black coffee and gave me something to eat and got me sobered up. Then we had a real long talk . . .

"You know," Hansen continued after a reflective pause, "I don't remember a word of what she said. I just remember that she took the time to listen, to care. Phyllis really cared. Me and my sisters could go up there, talk, play cards, whatever. Even sometimes when her boyfriend was there—my mother told you about Kurt, right?"

I nodded.

"He was nice to us, too. He was bright like her. He seemed to be interested in everything. He was into coin collecting and so was I, so we had something in common. He'd bring me his duplicates sometimes and we'd talk about coins. Numismatics is what Phyllis called it. That's a real crossword-puzzle word. Phyllis loved big words. Kurt too. They used to use big words all the time."

Kurt used to make exotic drinks—"You know," Hansen said, "the kind with lots of fruit in them"—and sometimes they would invite the youngsters upstairs for a "cocktail party." Kurt would transform the table into a makeshift

112

bar, wrap a towel around his waist, and play bartender, concocting elaborate drinks topped with oranges and lemons and maraschino cherries.

He'd pass one to Phyllis, who would taste it like a connoisseur, sniffing and swirling and smacking her lips. "We'd all laugh," Hansen said, smiling. Then Kurt would make the kids a drink leaving out the liquor and they'd drink them down greedily. "We used to have a good time," Hansen said. "But then I guess my mom told you, he just stopped coming. Just like that. No explanation, no nothing. It was too bad, because I liked the guy, and Phyllis was crazy about him. After he stopped coming, she just fell apart.

"She used to have real nice clothes, but after that she didn't take care of them, and she started getting real messy. Didn't comb her hair, didn't shower. You know, sloppy. I'd see her out walking on the streets with her head down, real sad. She looked all bent over and old. I had to feel sorry for her. She seemed so alone."

Phyllis turned to the church.

"Phyllis wasn't the kind to talk God and religion and all," Evelyn Hansen told me. "But she did pray and in her room there were lots of saints and things. I couldn't really tell you which saints they were. To me, I'm a Protestant you know, a saint is a saint. That's all I know on that subject, but I know she got some help from the Catholic church down the street. They gave her food and money sometimes. It helped her get by."

A block from the Hansens' home Our Lady of Angels Roman Catholic Church hulks like a sentinel keeping watch over the spiritual needs of Bay Ridge. It is an imposing red-brick structure, one of the largest churches in Brooklyn, with a congregation of about 20,000—rich and poor, but mostly middle class—whose tithes have placed rose windows overlooking the sacristy, a huge resonant pipe organ in the choir loft, and plush red-velvet curtains on the confessionals.

Day after day, Evelyn Hansen said, Phyllis would leave her quiet room on 76th Street and walk the streets of Bay Ridge until she found her way back to the cool, cavernous comfort of Our Lady of Angels Church.

As I sat in one of its long, polished-oak pews it was not hard to imagine her there too, kneeling, clenching rosary beads, hoping to heal herself under the gilded blue ceiling that bespoke the solidity, stability, and permanence that eluded her.

"I don't know how much money she was getting from the church, of course," Evelyn Hansen said. "Phyllis would never discuss it. But I know she was getting some help on a regular basis for quite a while."

If records were kept of this charity they were discarded long ago. No one at the church now remembers the disheveled, disoriented woman who came there to pray each day. But that was nearly twenty years ago; few of the staff went back that far and most of the priests hadn't even entered seminary then.

I managed to track the former pastor to a church in Far Rockaway, Queens, but he did not remember a Phyllis Iannotta. "It was a very long time ago," he said, "and I cannot recall this particular woman. But if she had come to us asking for help, we wouldn't have turned her away. Perhaps no records of that were ever kept, perhaps the priests simply gave her money or food or whatever, I really couldn't say. Over the years we helped many people informally with money for food or emergencies. We can't always get to know them personally."

Perhaps they did not really try; more likely, Phyllis would not let them. Her mind was deteriorating, slipping into the incurable disease doctors would later diagnose as schizophrenia. She would want to reach out to others but be unable to connect.

"The emptiness of daily living is exacerbated by the schizophrenic's need to withdraw from relationships," write Drs. Kayla F. Bernheim and Richard R. J. Lewine in their book *Schizophrenia: Symptoms, Causes, Treatments*. "The schizophrenic tends to be frightened of emotional intimacy," yet "at the same time, like all of us, the schizophrenic longs for close, satisfying relationships."

As the disease progresses, schizophrenics' emotions "flatten" and they become "lethargic, withdrawn and unmotivated." They may "hear voices . . . when no one is speaking" or "smile or giggle inappropriately, become incensed for no apparent reason or appear depressed and tearful during happy circumstances." Ultimately, "fantasy and reality can become hopelessly intertwined."

As time progressed, Phyllis became like a stranger. Within two years of Popeye's arrival and Kurt's abrupt departure, she was no longer "regular" or "vivacious" or even "brainy." She was none of the things Evelyn Hansen had liked and admired about her. It was as if she were no longer Phyllis, changed, someone else, someone barely recognizable. It was as if part of her were dead.

She told Evelyn Hansen that she was cold from the inside out, cold and numb.

Phyllis's symptoms developed late in life. Generally, the risk of schizophrenia declines sharply after the age of fifty—she was fifty-one by now—with most initial hospitalizations occurring in adolescence and young adulthood. Neither Philip nor Evelyn Hansen knew anything about schizophrenia. At first they believed, as perhaps did Phyllis herself, that she was suffering the effects of menopause—complicated by her breakup with Kurt. That made her illness easier to accept. But as Phyllis's behavior became increasingly bizarre, it became impossible to explain it away simply as a "change of life."

"I started getting real worried about her," Evelyn Hansen said. "She was acting sort of crazy. Like she was 'out there.' " She waved her hand as if to take in another galaxy. "She stopped eating altogether. All she'd take was honey and vinegar. That's all. It was some sort of fad diet. I'm telling you she ate nothing else. Just honey and vinegar. Imagine! The whole second floor stank of it. God, I'll never forget that smell.

"Phyllis was my friend," she continued. "I wanted to be a good friend to her, but we could only put up with so much." She folded her arms defensively across her chest. "We carried her for a full year. That's right, one whole year—fifty-two weeks—without asking for rent. Not a cent. I would say to Bob, 'Bob,' I would say, 'we gotta wait till Phyllis gets back on her feet.' But you could see that that might be a long, long time. And in the meantime, Bob was working two jobs and he would say, 'What am I bustin' my butt for anyway?' And to tell the truth, I just didn't have an answer for that one . . ."

The Russells, the other second-floor tenants, also were upset about Phyllis and her increasingly bizarre behavior.

"They complained about her. They knew she wasn't paying her rent and they let us know that if Phyllis left they'd take up her apartment. And they *could* pay."

I found Maryann Russell living in a spacious new apartment in Bensonhurst. She hadn't known about the murder. "That's terrible. Horrible," she said. "She was homeless, huh? A whatchacallit? A bag lady?"

I nodded.

"Well, that's a shame. But you know what they say. Them people don't want a real place to live. They actually prefer to live outside. That's a fact."

I held my tongue.

"She was kind of strange," Maryann Russell said. "Nice enough, I guess, but real strange. She was real quiet, never said much except hello. She kept to herself, if you know what I mean. I guess she was there a year before she invited me into her place—and the only thing that separated us was French doors. After that, we'd have coffee once in a while, maybe play a game of 500 rummy now and again. That's all. She didn't have no visitors or nothing, except sometimes her boyfriend, who I only saw maybe once or twice—he seemed like a nice fella—and the kids from downstairs. We never had no bad words or nothing."

"I heard she had some odd habits you didn't like," I ventured.

Her lips tightened defensively. Then she shrugged. The words spilled out in an angry stream. "Well, if Evelyn told you she was dirty, that was true. Of course I didn't like that. I mean she looked like an unmade bed half the time and she'd leave dirty dishes in our bathtub—we shared the bathtub—so you couldn't take a shower. And the whole damn place smelled like vinegar. Did Evelyn tell you about the vinegar? Phew! Some crazy diet she was on. I don't know. It could drive you crazy. I think it maybe made her a little crazy, that's for sure. I spoke to her about it, but it was like talking to the wall."

She rose from her chair, indicating that our conversation had come to an end. "Understand, we didn't exactly *push* for Phyllis to go," she said, walking me to the door. "We just told Evelyn that *if* she were to go, we'd take the room and, naturally, we'd pay extra . . ."

"I Am
Human
Too"

It all happened quietly. Phyllis was told to move out. She cried. Evelyn Hansen cried. Phyllis had lived in the house on 76th Street for more than ten years. Richard had grown to manhood. Little Kenneth, who was only a few months old when she moved in, was now in fifth grade. The girls, Janice, Susan, and Audrey, would soon be young women. Phyllis had watched them grow, helped them learn to read, nurtured them. She loved them all, and they loved her.

The Hansens had found Phyllis a new apartment only a few blocks away. There wasn't much to move: clothing, a few pots and pans, some bedding, and, of course, her pictures of saints, her popsicle-stick cathedral, and her boxes of books. Bob Hansen lugged it all downstairs, loaded it into his car, and drove the four blocks to the new apartment on the first floor of an old walkup at 7615 Third Avenue.

He piled the boxes around Phyllis in the large, empty room. Neither said a word. He drove off and returned with a maple bedroom set. "We didn't need it anymore," Evelyn Hansen said, "and she didn't have any furniture, so we thought it might, you know, help a bit . . ."

She spoke as if her conscience still bothered her. But, in truth, the Hansens were probably Phyllis's best friends, even as they were putting her out of their home. Popeye, who retreated into bars rather than face his sister's breakdown, wasn't around to help with the move. But nearly twenty years later, during one of our meetings at Kilroy's, he added a detail the Hansens had neglected to mention:

"They was tops to us," he said of the Hansens. "Sure they put her out. When you come right down to it, they didn't have no choice in the matter, right? And you know what they done? They paid her rent at the new place. That's right. One full month."

Phyllis gradually adjusted to her new home. She put up curtains, hung pictures, found corners for her knickknacks. Neighbors remember hearing her whistling and singing as she busied herself around the apartment. It seemed the change had done her good. It was 1965, and for the next decade Phyllis enjoyed a life of moderate improvement.

Her brother was earning some money as a handyman in local bars. He continued to live with her, and one day he brought home a new addition to the family—an old, fat tavern mongrel Phyllis dubbed Poochinello, a pun on the Italian word for clown. The three of them seemed happy together. "Sometimes Phyllis would come back over to see me just for a chat or to play cards," Evelyn Hansen said.

"She seemed fine, better, as if she was over whatever it was that was bothering her."

Within a year of moving into the first-floor apartment at 7615 Third Avenue, Phyllis was back to work again, this time, her Social Security file shows, as an hourly worker at Lutheran Medical Center and as a part-time employee of the New York City Board of Education. No records remain to indicate what her jobs were, but most likely they were as a clerk or perhaps as a cook or kitchen helper, jobs similar to ones she had held before.

By 1968, her reported earnings had risen to nearly $3,200 a year—not much, certainly, but nearly double the amount she had made in 1956, which until then had been her best year. The good fortune lasted only a year, however. By 1969, Phyllis was jobless again. The records offer no explanation. She may well have lost her job to her illness. For, as Bernheim and Lewine note, schizophrenics often quit work because they feel lonely or alienated, or get fired because of their expressions of anger or jealousy, even though they seem to be well.

In any case, Phyllis struggled along for a time on unemployment insurance and, Evelyn Hansen told me, occasional off-the-books work. By 1973, she had a steady job again, this time as a records clerk at the Brooklyn welfare office.

Two years later she was once again on the unemployment line. This time she had plenty of company.

It was 1975, and the City of New York was finally being made to pay the piper for years of credit-card financing. As the city staggered closer and closer to default, two city hospitals were forced to close, education programs were eliminated, the doors were closed on drug-treatment centers. Thousands of police officers were laid off. Firefighters were forced to work double shifts. All told, 30,000 municipal workers lost their jobs. Phyllis was one of them.

That same year, her illness, dormant for a decade, re-awakened. She fell apart. This time, there was nothing gradual about it. Within only a few months, she would be reduced to a raving madwoman: alternately shrinking in corners and exploding in tantrums, setting fires and holding delusional conversations with the dead.

Today, what used to be Phyllis's apartment on the ground floor of 7615 Third Avenue is occupied by a crafts store, and no one is left in the building who remembers her except Jackie Brady, a young housewife, who lives on the second floor.

She answered my knock with a baby in her arms. She looked tired and frazzled and in no mood to talk to a stranger. But, yes, she said, she did remember Phyllis Iannotta. "How could I ever forget *that* crazy lady?" She eyed me suspiciously. "What's your interest in her, anyway?" she demanded.

I told her about the murder. "I'm sorry," she said. "I didn't know." She stepped back and motioned me into the apartment. "I don't like to speak ill of the dead," she said, "but Phyllis *was* pretty strange. She always wore this long dirty sweater. Very dirty. She was like a witch who lived in a dark, dank dungeon. You could smell it when she opened the door. Whew! It was awful." She made a face. "I was afraid of her. Everybody was. She used to set fires. It was scary. She did it a couple of times that I can remember. Once we had to call the fire department."

Brady remembered that the smoke woke her.

"It was real late and I smelled something funny, so I got up and there was smoke coming from under her door. I got scared and ran out and the whole place was full of smoke. You could see it was coming from her apartment. Everybody was out in the hallway and somebody tried the door but it was locked so they called the fire department.

"When the firemen came she wouldn't open the door for them. She just kept screaming for them to go away. They were just getting ready to break the door down when she finally opened it and let them in." It was only a small fire, confined to an old chair, and the firemen easily put it out. "But it scared the hell out of us, I'll tell you that," Brady said. "We kept wondering what the old lady would do next."

She thought for a moment. "You should really talk to Frank Jaklic. He lived right next door to her. I bet he could tell you a thing or two. He lives in Manhattan now . . ."

I found Jaklic in the phone book. He was living in an apartment in Hell's Kitchen, not far from the Dwelling Place. I dialed the number.

"Oh sure, I remember her," he said. "She was sort of my initiation to New York. I was just a kid then, about twenty-five I guess, and straight from Michigan. I didn't know what to make of her. But I'll tell you this, after a little of her, I was ready for anything New York had to offer!"

He laughed. "That's not really fair. She could be a very nice lady, very pleasant really. But she had these radical mood swings. One minute she'd be pleasant, the next she'd be screaming about something. And I mean screaming. She had this darkness inside her that was incredible . . ." He paused, remembering.

"She was fascinating, just fascinating. She did all these *crazy* things. I mean, it wasn't just the fires. She did other things, too. Crazy stuff. Like, she'd hang her clothes out on the line and then just keep them there like an outdoor clothes closet. She'd just pull them off the line when she needed them. Sometimes, they'd be out there for like a week or two at a time. They'd get rained on, dirty, whatever. She'd wear them anyway. You'd see the dirt marks where the clothespins had been.

"You might call that just a"—he searched for the right word—"a quirk, I guess you could say. An eccentricity. But there were other things that showed she was, well, sick, you know, mentally ill."

Jaklic explained: "We shared access to a little backyard. By Michigan standards it would hardly count for anything. But in New York, in New York that little piece of green ground counted for a lot. Phyllis always let her dog go out there and things got really messy. So I put up a fence to divide the yard—half for her and half for me. I thought that was fair.

"Well, one day I was out there cleaning up my half when she ran out into the yard screaming, 'Those are *my* rocks! What are you doing with *my* rocks?' I was dumbfounded. I didn't know what to say. She told me those rocks—these were just ordinary, regular, garden-variety rocks, believe me—she said they were worth a fortune and I had better keep my hands off them. So, what the heck, I just collected all her precious rocks and dropped them over the fence." He chuckled.

"Then, one morning, this was some time after the rock

thing, I woke up and saw Phyllis out in the backyard. It was pouring rain, but she was on her knees with her hands raised to the sky. You know what she was doing?" He paused for effect. "She was exorcising spirits. You got it. Chasing away devils. Pret-ty spoo-ky. It went on like that for three days and three nights in the pouring rain. On the fourth day, her brother came home and found her on her knees babbling. I talked to other people in the building and they didn't know what to make of her either. I guess" Jaklic said, "we all just thought of her as the resident nut."

Phyllis, too, may have watched herself with a mixture of horror and confusion. For typically, schizophrenics stand outside themselves, detach themselves, and watch their own deterioration.

"The schizoid individual exists under the black sun, the evil eye, of his own scrutiny," psychiatrist R. D. Laing writes in *The Divided Self.* "The glare of his awareness kills his spontaneity, his freshness; it destroys all joy. Everything withers under it . . . the schizoid individual depersonalizes his relationship with himself. That is to say, he turns the living spontaneity of his being into something dead and lifeless by inspecting it."

Ultimately, many schizophrenics come to believe they are not real. One recovering patient described this depersonalization in *Psychiatry* magazine:

"It is so far from reality that in order to be made into a concrete real definition it has to be described in an abstract, unreal way, if it is to be fully understood. . . . The feeling itself is one of unworthiness, in the way that a counterfeit bill might feel when being examined by a banker with a good understanding and appreciation of real currency . . . like watching a movie based on a play and, having once seen the play, realizing that the movie is just a description of it and one that brings back memories and yet isn't real and just different enough to make all the difference. . . . The important things have left and the unimportant things stay behind, making the loss more apparent by their presence."

What, I wondered, would Popeye remember of all this? I found him sitting in the middle of the bar at Kilroy's, his head propped in his hand in front of a drink, just as he had been the first night I saw him, just as he was virtually every night. But that night he was feeling talkative. He told me about his picks at Off-Track Betting, about when the subway was a nickel ("You're too young to remember that, but when we was kids . . ."), about one of the girls at the bookstore who he said told him he was cute ("I tells her, honey, not tonight. I got a headache. Helps to play hard-to-get"). We both laughed.

He finished his beer. I ordered another round.

"Tell me, Phil," I started, "about the time your sister Fay was out in the backyard talking to spirits. What was that all about?"

He shook his head. "If I was to tell you," he said, "you wouldn't believe it." He took a sip of his beer.

"Try me."

"Well," he said, "it was like this. It was back in the place on Third Avenue. I remember that she kept saying she was talkin' to our mom and dad. She was actin' crazy, like she was communicatin' with spirits or somepin'. It's one thing to talk to dead people, you know? It's a whole 'nother thing when they talk back . . .

"I dunno. It was all crazy. One minute she was talkin' about dead people, the next minute she was sayin' the bullies are out to get her or somepin'. It was all crazy stuff. Whaddya gonna do? She was goin' through the changes, see. You know, the whaddyacallit, the change of life, and that was making her crazy. I didn't know what the hell to do. So I called this friend of Fay's. Don't know what her name was. Can't remember. Good lady. Fay knew her for a long time, so's I called her."

Catherine Finstad, Phyllis's friend since their days in the Navy Yard thirty years before, said Philip's call came "out of the blue." She hadn't seen Phyllis for months and had no idea what had happened.

"He hemmed and hawed, and I couldn't figure what was going on. He was trying to say that she was going off the deep end, but he didn't know how to. I think he wanted to be loyal to her. Finally he just said Phyllis needed a friend real bad and he asked me to come over right away. I knew something was wrong and, of course, I went.

"It was pretty bad." Catherine Finstad's voice cracked. "I hadn't seen Phyllis in some time, and I just wasn't prepared for this. She was in a terrible state. I told her, 'You can't go on living like this,' and I tried to talk to her, but it didn't do much good. She kept saying the guys next door were trying to get her, and she was very suspicious of everything.

"Her apartment looked like the Collier brothers' basement and she had stopped eating. She was surviving on caffeine and nicotine. When I told her she had to eat and take better care of herself, she'd say, 'What do you care what I'm eating?' and she got very angry. It was just awful."

127

Finstad visited her old friend regularly in the weeks that followed. But it seemed to do little good. Phyllis seemed to be getting sicker and sicker. She recalled one visit in particular:

"One time I went over and she was hallucinating. Sometimes she thought she saw Jesus and the Blessed Mother. When I tried to talk to her she accused me of everything you could think of. She said she knew I had been upstairs all the time with her neighbors plotting against her. She said to me, 'I would know your voice anywhere,' and she said my son—Johnny was her godson, remember—was up there too. That really hurt . . ." She paused and shielded her eyes with her hand. "You see," she continued a few seconds later, "Johnny had an accident three weeks before and he died."

Finstad had to stop speaking for a moment to compose herself. "I'm sorry," she said. "That was a very difficult time for me. You know, with Phyllis and my boy all at the same time. Phyllis didn't know. We kept it from her because of the state she was in."

Finstad left Phyllis late that night. "She seemed a little better. Almost as if she were exhausted, you know, worn out. I hoped things might be getting better."

But the next morning, Philip phoned her in a panic. "He said things were really bad and he didn't know what to do. Poor guy. I felt sorry for him because he wanted to do right by her but he just didn't know how. I was pretty worried and I didn't really know what to do either. So I called a couple of organizations for advice and they suggested I take her to Lutheran Medical Center. I called them, and they said they would take her. But only if she came voluntarily."

Finstad had no idea just how big a problem that would be.

"Me and my husband John drove over to Phyllis's hoping to take her right to Lutheran. But it wasn't that simple. Oh no. Phyllis was a wreck, all agitated and fearful. She was wearing this dirty old dress with religious medals pinned all over it. She was all disheveled. She said she saw my father's skull in her backyard. And she thought her parents were out there too. I tried to tell her they were just a couple of old paper bags. But in her state, she just couldn't hear it. She was really cracking up.

"We tried for two or three hours to talk her into going, but she wouldn't have anything to do with it. She wouldn't even put her shoes on, and when we tried, she'd curl her toes so you couldn't get them on. I'm telling you, it was a big scene. Her brother, understandably, was all upset and frustrated and finally he took her and yelled at her, 'You're going to the hospital if I have to knock you out.' "

But it had no effect. Phyllis was not going to any hospital voluntarily.

"It was Philip who figured out how to get her into the car," Finstad continued. "He took us aside and said, 'Look, we're just going to have to lie to her. Tell her we're going to see little Johnny.' Well, like I said, Phyllis she didn't know he had passed away, so when we said that she just calmed down and got into the car like nothing had happened."

They drove to Lutheran.

And then the screaming started. "You're not going to take me into that goddamned place! Get your fucking hands offa me! You can go to hell. All of you. No! Get away! Leave me be!" Philip and John Finstad grabbed Phyllis under her arms and pulled her out of the car. She kicked at them, scratched at them with long, dirty fingernails, and tried to bite their hands.

A small crowd formed as they dragged her toward the massive yellow-brick hospital. She latched onto a wrought-iron fence and her fingers had to be pried off one by one, and still she fought. Finally, the two men managed to drag her through the hospital doors into a crowded waiting room. And, as Phyllis continued to scream obscenities, a nurse patiently explained that there were no doctors who could see her right now. "Perhaps you ought to take her to Kings County Hospital," she suggested.

"I thought I was going to collapse," Finstad said. "It was like a nightmare. It took forever for an ambulance to come from Kings County, and by the time it arrived Phyllis was completely nuts. She had to be taken out in handcuffs." Finstad waited at Kings County Hospital until five in the morning before the doctors made up their minds to have Phyllis committed. "By then I was ready to be taken to the bughouse myself."

Phyllis was "2PCed"—committed on a "two-physician certificate," a document signed by a pair of psychiatrists who must determine that the patient is potentially homicidal or suicidal, the only reasons under New York State law a person can be committed to a psychiatric hospital involuntarily.

As soon as the papers were signed, white-jacketed attendants dragged Phyllis down the tiled corridor and out of sight.

Finstad shuddered at the memory: "She kept shouting, 'Jezebel!' at me as if I was the worst person in the world. It was such an ordeal, like walking through the fires of hell.

And this after my boy died. I'm telling you I'm still not over it." She placed her head in her hands and couldn't speak for a minute or more.

Phyllis was at Kings County only four days before doctors decided she required more intensive treatment. On September 3, 1975, she was transferred to South Beach Psychiatric Center, then a new hospital spread out over fifty acres on Staten Island, where she would be one of about 300 patients.

Dr. Anthony Pietro-Pinto, chief psychiatrist at Lutheran Medical Center, ushered me into a tiny office cluttered with books and journals and, interestingly, dozens of unicorns. There were pictures of unicorns on every wall. Figures of them in plastic and plaster and glass adorned every bookshelf. On his desk was a stuffed toy unicorn. What, I wondered, would Dr. Freud have had to say about that?

Pietro-Pinto motioned me into a chair and pulled a thick manila folder from under a pile of papers. "I think this is what you've come for," he said. "I hope you'll find it helpful."

It had taken me a year to locate Phyllis's psychiatric records (she had been an outpatient at Lutheran after her discharge from South Beach) and longer still to convince authorities to let me see them.

I opened the folder and began to read, only partially aware that the doctor was still talking. "I did not know the patient," he was saying, "and her doctor is no longer in the state, but if you need any help translating the jargon let me know."

My mind was in the file, and I said nothing. He had the courtesy not to be offended. "I'll leave you alone then to look things over," he offered. "Holler if you need me."

But the file spoke for itself. Eloquently.
It began with the admitting physician's report:

WARD: 064

TIME: 2 p.m.

CHIEF COMPLAINT (IN PATIENT'S OWN WORDS IF POSSIBLE): "I am human too."

Eviction

The admitting psychiatrist had dutifully copied Phyllis's lament onto the printed form and added his own observations: "Disheveled, labile woman who is guarded and evasive. Denies history of any problems. . . . Silly grin at times. Speech loose and autistic. . . . No suicidal or homicidal ideations. . . . Insight and judgment poor."

"There's nothing wrong with me," she told the doctor repeatedly. "I don't need to be in this hospital."

"Schizophrenia, paranoid type." He scrawled the words in the blank that required Phyllis be given a label, and recommended she be given electroshock treatment or psychotropic drugs.

Phyllis remained at South Beach Psychiatric for exactly one month. In that time, she underwent individual psychotherapy three times a week, group therapy four times a week, and was placed in art therapy classes and a women's social group.

She was also given 500 milligrams a day of Thorazine, a powerful tranquilizer that diminishes anger and fear and helps schizophrenics control their hallucinations and delusional thinking.

The records show that Phyllis suffered from "anxiety, fears, phobias, social withdrawal, suspicion and persecution." In an early interview, one of her therapists noted that Phyllis was "overfriendly" and "overdemonstrative," but at the same time "guarded." Asked a simple question, she might begin, "Well, I'll tell you . . ." then balk and say, "No, maybe I shouldn't, you know everything anyway." She sometimes started laughing for no apparent reason.

The therapist said Phyllis's movements were "fast and rigid." She was nervous and had developed a stutter. She told her doctor her neighbors were out to get her. She was not very specific. Throughout the month a team of therapists, social workers, and doctors were able to glean only the sketchiest account of what had brought her to them:

"Approximately six months ago, patient made requests to her landlord to have her apartment painted. Each request was answered with a negative response. At the same time, patient was laid off from her job [with the Brooklyn welfare office]. . . . Patient's relationship with brother is minimal. Her only source of support (mentally) is her girlfriend [Catherine Finstad]. . . . In combining these happenings with no one for support, it appears that the patient became increasingly agitated, was not able to sleep and began to have auditory hallucinations."

Phyllis told the doctor nothing about her worries over Philip, and she kept her relationship with Kurt a secret.

"No male friends since 15 years ago," he noted after one of their sessions. "No sex since 15 years ago. Never married because took care of parents and never cared for anyone that much. Longest relationship 1½ years." He also wrote: "No history of setting fires." Phyllis, as always, kept her self to herself.

On October 3, 1975, one month to the day after she was dragged screaming and struggling down the hospital's antiseptic corridors, she was discharged from South Beach Psychiatric with a prescription for 500 milligrams of Thorazine a day, a large dosage.

Her discharge papers portray a changed woman. After a month at South Beach, her record indicates she was "a neatly dressed woman who relates to interviewer in a friendly, cooperative manner. Her speech is fast at times but with minimal stuttering. Denies homicidal/suicidal ideation. Judgment is good. Appears to have gained minimal insight." Her condition, according to the record, had "improved."

But improved is not cured. There is no cure for schizophrenia, only treatment. And, while some schizophrenics respond so well to treatment that they are able to function with little risk of repeat episodes, others never attain a long-term ability to function independently. Phyllis's recovery was short-lived.

After her first visit to the Lutheran Medical outpatient clinic, the doctor wrote: "Patient is a short, slightly obese female dressed in slacks and sweater. Gray hair. Mood calm, affect appropriate. No overt thought disorder. Not homicidal or suicidal. Good memory. Judgment, insight limited." That was three days after her release from South Beach. Ten months later, the hospital files revealed, Phyllis had become "frequently confused and disoriented" and was unable to deal with even such basic matters as paying the utility company without the support of a psychiatric social worker.

I tried to make out the signature on the bottom of the notes. Linda Trentmen? Trolman? I took the folder to Dr. Pietro-Pinto. "Trotman," he said. "Linda Trotman. She's a psychiatric social worker. One of the best. I think you're in luck. She's still here with us." He flipped through his Rolodex, wrote down a telephone number, and handed it to me. "Let me talk to her first," he said. "Sort of clear the way for you."

Trotman and I met a week later over tea in her book-filled apartment in a building not far from Dewey Junior High, Phyllis's alma mater. She was an attractive, intelligent woman in her midthirties, and was saddened, but not surprised, by the news I brought her.

"Phyllis was a very sick woman," she told me. "After a while she just stopped coming to the clinic. We tried to track her down, but we weren't able to locate her. I'm not particularly surprised that she became a bag lady. It's very sad, but I suppose in some ways it was predictable. She had no real support system, no real friends. Lack of friendships, intimate relationships, characterized her life at that point and I felt that would be a problem. She had a brother, but he wasn't much help, I gathered."

Trotman paused, sipped her tea and collected her thoughts. "Even then Phyllis used to carry all her papers in a shopping bag. She would lug one bag, sometimes two, to every session. She would come to the clinic dressed in layers of dirty clothes. She always wore pants under her skirts and her clothing was always disheveled. Sometimes

136

she would cut out portions of her shoes so her bare feet protruded. They were filthy.

"Her hygiene was really awful. She was frequently smelly, so smelly that I had to talk to her about it. It's a very delicate subject, a difficult topic to broach with a patient, but, you know, I had to spend a lot of time with this woman. The clinic sessions lasted at least forty-five minutes, sometimes longer. I might spend eight hours with her if we had to go out to a social agency, say welfare, or something. I couldn't have her going like that. And, frankly, I found it just too unpleasant to ignore."

At first, Trotman said, Phyllis made up excuses for her dirtiness. "She would say her tub was too small, she didn't have any hot water, things like that. But I continued to discuss it with her and ultimately she bathed. The lack of hygiene was the only aggressive or hostile form of behavior I saw from Phyllis—a kind of safe hostility, I guess you could say. Oh, sure, she could get agitated sometimes, like when she would talk about her layoff, but that wasn't inappropriate. No, at that stage, I wouldn't call Phyllis an angry woman. She was anxious, but not angry most of the time."

Phyllis was one of about thirty patients Trotman, then a therapist with about two years' experience, was handling. She usually met with four patients a day in the tiny cluttered office she shared with other social workers at the clinic.

Trotman laughed. "It was always 'musical offices' with all of us kind of scrambling for a place to meet our clients. This wasn't Park Avenue where you go lie on a couch. I dealt mostly with the patients' social problems, getting them to appointments, helping them through the difficulties of dealing with people, making sure they understood dates and times and procedures. Sometimes I'd schlepp with them to Social Security or Welfare, that sort of thing.

"Phyllis was in better shape than many of them. She was a bright woman and interesting to talk to. She had a sense of humor, too, but she didn't smile often. She was anxious a lot, and careworn. You'd see that in her face, just weary, drained dry. She was very sick, but she had some insight into her illness. She understood she was sick. I would say, in general, that she handled herself very well—as long as she wasn't confronted with anything too upsetting."

But life for Phyllis, like many of the troubled poor, was one upset after another.

While Phyllis was in the hospital, her landlord had moved everything from her apartment. "I'll never forget it," her former neighbor Frank Jaklic told me. "There was tons of junk in there and the landlord had to use a snow shovel to dig out the dirt and crud. It was a mess."

"We all panicked," Catherine Finstad said. "Phyllis did not know what to do, and neither, really, did we. She had no place to go. We were all afraid this would really do her in."

Hospital officials contacted a judge in landlord-tenant court. Informally, he advised that it would be quicker and simpler to find Phyllis a new home than to go to court with what might be a losing case.

Miraculously, in only a few weeks Finstad managed to find a new apartment for Phyllis on the second floor of an attractive red-brick building at 7311 Fourth Avenue, only a few blocks from her former place. It was larger and brighter than her old apartment; Phyllis seemed to like it. Her doctors, convinced it would be a long time, if ever, before she could go back to work, encouraged her to apply to Social Security for Supplemental Security Income, government aid for those too disabled to work. Phyllis could easily pay her rent once she began receiving her SSI checks. No one doubted her eligibility.

But twenty days after her discharge, Phyllis received a terse rejection. On the form, a Social Security bureaucrat had written:

"Medical evidence in file establishes significant impairment, however not one that precludes her from doing her customary work. Therefore, claim is denied."

No matter that Phyllis's doctors had certified her emotionally unstable and recommended she not work. No matter that she still believed her neighbors, even her friends, were plotting against her. The Social Security Administration officially determined that Phyllis *could* work. They suggested she apply for welfare.

The real reason for the turndown had nothing to do with Phyllis's ability to work. In fact, it had little to do with Phyllis. It had to do with money. Social Security benefits are paid with federal dollars. Welfare is paid with a combination of state and city money. When money is tight, everyone looks for someone else to spend it. What had happened was a tactic familiar to social workers: a Brooklyn Social Security bureaucrat had passed the buck. Phyllis went on welfare. Her entitlement was $246 a month. Despite her illness, she was now required to meet with a city job counselor and go on job interviews. If she failed to do so, she would be dropped from the welfare rolls.

"It was difficult for Phyllis to be collecting welfare after she had worked in a welfare office," Trotman said. "She saw the irony in it and sometimes it made her angry. But also, you know, welfare doesn't help people much with their self-image. At welfare—particularly in tough fiscal times—the assumption is you're trying to cheat. They can really put you down, make it difficult to get what you're entitled to, make you feel ashamed, treat you like a criminal. And they have no feelings. Of course, this stress took its toll on Phyllis's mental health . . ."

In February 1976, Phyllis again sought money from the Social Security Administration, this time for retirement benefits. She was sixty-two, the age of eligibility. But once again a man behind a desk labored for months to keep her from getting that money. Her Social Security dossier is thick with correspondence aimed at discrediting her claim. One document in the file describes the problem:

"Wage earner called at office with . . . mental health worker. She insisted she was born May 8, 1914. Her birth certificate was obviously altered. . . . Claimant states that on her first Social Security card [issued in 1938] her correct date of birth was listed. She had a vague memory and proof of age will be difficult. She has sent [to Italy] for her original birth certificate—in spite of her allegations, I believe her birth certificate will show 1924."

It was Phyllis's own fault. In 1946, when she had applied for a second Social Security card, she had shaved ten years off her age. "I wanted people at work to think that I was younger than I really was," she explained in a written statement to the Social Security Administration. Now, thirty years later, she was paying the price of vanity. Ultimately, Phyllis's birth certificate would bear out her story; Social Security would grant her her retirement benefits. But this battle also took its toll.

On her next clinic visit, her doctor noted that she was "labile and nervous." She refused to take her Thorazine.

"Phyllis stopped taking her medicine altogether," Cath-

140

erine Finstad remembers. "She really needed that medicine, and when she stopped taking it she started acting crazy again. I tried to talk to her about it, to tell her how important it was, but she'd always get very suspicious. 'What's it matter to you?' she'd say. 'What's in it for you?' Sometimes, she'd tell me the medicine was giving her a rash. So I'd say, 'Go get another prescription.' But of course, she never did."

Thorazine can be as horrible as it is wonderful. At best it can leave those who take it lethargic and unmotivated. At worst it causes them to develop uncontrollable movements of the mouth and neck. And somewhere in the middle is another, strange, problem with the drug: For many schizophrenics it takes away the mystical euphoria they sometimes feel at the height of their insanity.

The intense alternating feelings of schizophrenia can be painful and damaging, but as Bernheim and Lewine note, "they can also be extremely exciting," so that "given the choice between the emptiness of a schizophrenic's sanity and the rich variety of his madness, we would experience great difficulty in committing ourselves to sanity."

Whatever the reason, Phyllis was no longer taking her Thorazine. Her sickness could only get worse.

Troubled and unable to function well without her medication, she failed to show up for a routine employment conference and was determined ineligible for welfare. It didn't matter that Phyllis was clearly too sick to work. The rule would not bend: to collect welfare one had to look for work. Employees in the same welfare office where she had been a records clerk not long before told her there was nothing they could do. They stamped her records "Failure to Comply." And that was that.

A few days later, the psychiatric records reveal, Phyllis

arrived at Trotman's office "very confused and disoriented." The young therapist called welfare and tried to smooth things over, but the man on the other end of the phone was firm. "Try SSI again," he told her. "She's not getting welfare."

More forms were filled out. One gave the government the right to "contact any third parties necessary to process my Social Security claim"; another allowed authorities to override privacy restrictions in their search for evidence of her disability. Forms were sent to government agencies to confirm information she volunteered. For months paper changed hands. But none of it was currency.

Phyllis was no longer able to pay her rent. She could not afford to eat more than one meal a day. Finally, her doctor wrote the Social Security Administration. Phyllis, he said, was attending therapy sessions but "she refuses medications. She needs medication and we are trying to persuade her. She is chronically disabled." He explained some of her history. Finally, he wrote: "Her prognosis is poor." The letter was dated December 3, 1976.

Christmas came and went. Phyllis never noticed. She was too busy falling apart.

The apartment house at 7311 Fourth Avenue where Phyllis lived is a sturdy four-story red-brick building, in the style of the early 1940s. It has a small lawn in front with some scraggly shrubbery that hints at someone's efforts to maintain the building's place in the middle-class respectability of the neighborhood. It is directly across from Our Lady of Angels Church, but by the time Phyllis moved there she was no longer worshiping in its polished pews or seeking handouts from its clergy. Still, Catherine Finstad told me,

Phyllis enjoyed watching weddings and confirmations from her window on the third floor.

The doors to the lobby were locked when I went there, but I hung around until someone left, then slipped through the door before it closed. There was no one in the lobby. I looked around. Hardly luxurious. But solid. Clean, well tended. I walked up the landing and looked at the names on the door, picked one at random, and knocked.

I hated this part, the part where you wait for a someone to come to the door, someone who's going to think you're trying to sell him something or take something away from him. It is something reporters do all the time, of course. But that makes it only a little easier. In New York, people don't like strangers to knock on their doors. It has a tendency to make them hostile.

A dog barked loudly. A woman behind the door shouted mild obscenities at him in a futile attempt to shut him up. She opened the door a crack. A German shepherd's head emerged. The woman's knuckles were white where they grasped his collar. "Yes?"

I told her I was with the *Daily News* and I was doing a story on a woman who had lived in the building and did she remember a Phyllis Iannotta? It all came out fast; the dog rushed my delivery.

The woman yanked the dog's collar. "Yes," she said, "I knew Phyllis. Knew her pretty well." I'd gotten lucky the first try. She asked if I'd like to come in. "He's okay," she said of the dog. "Just makes a lot of noise." She opened the door wider and I slipped past. The dog followed us into the living room. I sat down in an armchair and he put his head in my lap like we were old friends.

The woman told me her name was Maureen Evers.

"Phyllis used to live upstairs," she said. "Why are you writing about her?" I told her about the murder. She shrugged and nodded as if the news came as no surprise. "I knew she was living on the streets," she said. "That started after she left here. She did not leave here voluntarily, if you know what I mean. She was a very sick woman, very sick. They had to put her out.

"I don't know what was going on with her, poor woman. She used to leave all the hot water on—I mean, she'd turn on all the faucets in the apartment until the whole place was filled with steam. It was incredible. You'd see the steam billowing out the window. Something was wrong. She needed all that warmth.

"She used to set fires, too. It was pretty bad. She set a couple that I remember. Everybody complained about her. We all did. So the landlord wound up calling in a city marshal to evict her. But when the marshal came, she wouldn't come to the door. She pretended she wasn't there. I'm not usually one to side with the marshals, but this was too much. They had to get her out of there.

"The marshal called the cops and they were starting to drill the lock when she finally opened the door. She started yelling and screaming. She kept screaming 'You've got no right to do this, I've paid my rent.' Everybody knew she hadn't paid her rent in months. She had fought with the landlord about it. Well, anyway, the marshals got the cops and they took her away, I think to a hospital."

Evers said she didn't know what happened after that, only that Phyllis did not come back and that she had seen her wandering the streets with her brother.

"You ought to talk to Roger Leigh," she suggested. "He was Phyllis's downstairs neighbor. He knows more about what happened than I do. He was right in the middle of the whole mess." She left the room and returned with a phone number. "Give him a call," she said. "I'm sure he'll talk to you." The number had a New Jersey area code. I called the next morning.

Leigh defended the landlord. "He didn't have much choice but to evict her," he told me. "See, she'd really gone crazy. She'd set fires. We used to call her Phyllis the Flame."

He explained: "One night I was coming home, I guess it was about twelve-thirty or one in the morning, and I thought I smelled smoke. I started to investigate. I felt a little like a jerk sniffing at people's doors to find where the smoke was coming from, but I was worried, so I kept on checking. I was pretty sure it was coming from her apartment. I knocked. No answer. I knocked again. Still no answer, but I could hear her moving around in there and I could hear this crackling noise like a flame. Then I heard this sound like the tearing of paper. It was newspaper, you could tell by the length of the tear.

"I called to her, 'This is Roger, the guy with the dog downstairs. Let me in, I'll help you put it out.' But she shouted, 'Go away, mind your own business.' I tried talking to her through the door, but it was no use. By then, it was getting pretty smoky. I had to call the fire department.

"When the firemen came she let them right in, but she had already put water on the fire. I went into the apartment with the superintendent, and this is what she had done: she had set the fire in the kitchen sink and I guess she was just standing there, feeding the fire with newspaper and watching it get bigger and bigger. Kind of scary, huh?"

There were other fires. "It got to be a serious problem,"

Leigh said. "It was dangerous. We were scared she'd burn the place down. So we got the landlord to bring in the marshal. After they carted her away, he changed the locks to her apartment."

Phyllis could no longer get into her apartment, but she still had the key to the building. A few days later, Roger Leigh found her and Philip—"and that old dog of theirs"—asleep on the stairs in front of their old apartment. "I didn't know what to do," he said. "But I was afraid about her setting fires, so I told them they would have to leave. They refused, so I had to call the cops.

"The police came and took them away. They said they wanted to put her in the hospital, but, you know, because of legalities, because she wouldn't sign herself in, they couldn't commit her. So the two of them were back about an hour later, and we had a little run-in. This time I said if they didn't leave I would have to throw them out bodily. I walked them downstairs and I pushed them out the door, then I turned around and I hid behind the corner so I was out of sight and I waited there knowing that she would still have the key." He chuckled at his cleverness.

"Sure enough, a few minutes later the door starts opening. I come out around the corner, grab the door, pull it and yank the key right out of the lock. Then I pushed the two of them out of the door and kept the key." He shrugged. "This does sound terrible, I know. It sounds heartless. It was in the winter. You feel kind of bad putting these people out in the cold. Nevertheless you have to say to yourself, 'Am I more concerned about being a bad guy to them or am I concerned with the safety of my family?'

"I don't remember seeing her brother after that. But I'd see her in the area from time to time, just walking the streets. She didn't look too good, and she would be carrying these shopping bags filled with things . . ."

That was in February 1977. The temperature that month in the Borough of Brooklyn averaged 31 degrees Fahrenheit.

Nearly two years after she applied, the Social Security Administration saw its way clear to pay Phyllis $216 a month in SSI for her disability. But when the check arrived at 7311 Fourth Avenue, there was no one there to receive it.

Phyllis had disappeared into the streets of Brooklyn. No one—not her brother or her social worker, Linda Trotman, or her old friends, Catherine Finstad and Evelyn Hansen—could tell me how she survived the winter or for how long she lived without a roof over her head.

Philip had gone his own way and Phyllis's paranoia made it impossible for her to turn to anyone else. Even before she was evicted she had stopped going to the mental health clinic, and she no longer trusted her closest friends. "She came by one day screaming and shouting that my husband was getting the FBI after her," Evelyn Hansen recalled. "I never saw her after that." Catherine Finstad found Phyllis's condition so overwhelming that she had stopped visiting her "to keep my own sanity." When Phyllis lost her home, her friends lost track of her completely. "In a way," Hansen confessed, "I didn't want to know where she was."

Formula
for
Homelessness

Phyllis was alone. Yet she was one of thousands. Perhaps a million Americans, 36,000 of them New Yorkers, also had no home. It was a quiet catastrophe impelled not by war or famine or plague, but by the wholesale depopulation of mental hospitals, a chronic nationwide shortage of housing, and a drastic lack of jobs.

Nowhere had these upheavals combined more forcefully than in New York, where they created a 40 percent rise in homelessness in less than twenty years.

The numbers were staggering. From 1971 to 1977, the first year of Phyllis's homelessness, applications for admission to the Women's Shelter in Manhattan, at that time the only municipal shelter for women in the city, rose from 872 to 3,355. There were only forty-seven beds; 2,420 applications were rejected in 1977. Perhaps Phyllis was among those turned away. There is no record that she ever stayed there.

The shelter Phyllis needed most, of course, was a hospital. But no Samaritan noting her distress on the streets of Bay Ridge, no police officer or social worker even, could have had her committed. For at that time, the nation's mental health establishment was suffering its own special brand of insanity. It was called deinstitutionalization, and it was a good intention that paved the road to hell for countless thousands of mentally ill Americans.

Before it was over, nearly 400,000 patients would be purged from the mental wards of the nation's state hospitals, and thousands more who, like Phyllis, desperately needed treatment would find hospital doors closed to them.

Confused and disoriented, they were left to fend for themselves on city streets.

Deinstitutionalization began in the early 1960s in New York State, where more than 90,000 mental patients were crowded into twenty-three outmoded hospitals, most of them little more than warehouses where the insane were shelved and forgotten, even by their doctors. Whole wards at the notorious Manhattan State Psychiatric Center, for example, were said to be without nurses or psychiatric social workers, let alone psychiatrists.

Similar situations existed throughout the country, and everywhere word of Dickensian conditions had begun to filter from behind asylum walls: horror stories of patients who had been beaten and starved, drugged into oblivion or allowed to wallow uncared for in their own feces. There were accounts of deaths that went unreported—and possibly undetected—for days.

The public demanded reforms. Instead, they received a prescription: Thorazine, Stelazine, Haldol, lithium.

These and other psychotropic wonder drugs, able to control, if not cure, the crippling symptoms of mental illness, became thought of as panaceas—not only for patients but for an ailing system: patients need no longer be warehoused in "snakepit" hospitals; they could be treated at home.

A system was envisioned in which hospitals would function as acute-care facilities where most patients would be kept only long enough for their condition to be evaluated and their symptoms to be treated.

From the hospitals, patients, stabilized on drugs, would be released into the care of a network of smaller institutions in their own communities: halfway houses staffed by professionals, group homes with special services, or their own homes with support from outpatient clinics and counseling centers.

Phyllis's experience was typical. She was hospitalized for a month, then released to her apartment under the supervision of a psychiatric social worker. Arrangements were made for her to visit the outpatient clinic at Lutheran Medical Center for therapy and counseling and to have her dosage of Thorazine adjusted.

It is difficult to argue with the theory of deinstitutionalization. The ill effects of long-term hospitalization were well known: passivity, apathy, inability to function outside the institution. As one researcher noted, long hospitalizations "induce socialization experiences that prepare the individual to live successfully within the hospital; they have little relevance to inculcating social competencies that will enable him to cope with life outside the hospital."

Deinstitutionalization also promised an economic advantage. Outpatient care was cheaper and could be financed through Medicaid. Emptying the hospitals would shift the enormous financial burden—between $400 and $500 million a year in New York State alone—to the federal government.

So in 1965 New York State made deinstitutionalization a public policy and opened the doors of the asylums.

Between 1965 and 1978, the population of the state's mental hospitals dropped from 90,000 to 23,000. Supported by the Joint Commission on Mental Health, an independent body set up by Congress in 1955, deinstitutionalization soon became national policy; in those same thirteen years, the number of mental patients in state hospitals across the country dropped from about 560,000 to 193,000.

But the community mental health services—the backbone of the concept—never materialized, and deinstitutionalization rapidly dissolved into chaos.

Dr. M. Brewster Smith, a University of California psychologist who served as vice president of the Joint Commission in the 1960s, now concedes that "extravagant claims were made for the benefits of shifting from state hospitals to community clinics" and that "the professional community made mistakes and was overly optimistic."

"With the advantage of hindsight," an American Psychiatric Association study noted in 1984, "we can see that the era of deinstitutionalization was ushered in with much naïveté and many simplistic notions. . . . The importance of developing such fundamental resources as supportive living arrangements was often not clearly seen, or at least not implemented. 'Community treatment' was much discussed, but there was no clear idea as to what it should consist of, and the resistance of community mental health centers to providing services to the chronically mentally ill was not anticipated. Nor was it foreseen how reluctant many states would be to allocate funds for community-based services."

The result, says Dr. Jack R. Ewalt, a former director of the Joint Commission, "was like proposing a plan to build a new airplane and ending up only with a wing and a tail."

At the same time the states were clearing out their hospitals, the federal government, as a result of a series of court decisions meant to safeguard the civil rights of the mentally ill, was setting stricter standards on the kinds of patients who could be admitted to mental hospitals against their will.

Hailed as victories by patients' rights advocates, these rulings of the 1960s and 1970s remedied some of the terrible abuses in the public hospitals. But they also erected nearly insurmountable barriers to comprehensive care for the mentally ill. Aimed at abolishing unnecessary and punitive hospitalization, they stressed the patient's right to freedom even when independence conflicted with what doctors saw as the patient's best interest.

In *Lake v. Cameron*, for example, a U.S. appeals court ruled in 1966 that a patient could not be involuntarily hospitalized if an alternative that infringed less on his right to liberty could be found. Nine years later, in *O'Connor v. Donaldson*, the U.S. Supreme Court added that "a state cannot confine . . .a nondangerous person who is capable of surviving safely in freedom by himself or with the help of willing and responsible family members or friends."

In practical terms, these decisions were interpreted to mean that unless a person was a threat to himself or others—suicidal or homicidal—he couldn't be committed against his will.

The Donaldson case was particularly damaging. The 1984 study by the American Psychiatric Association explains: "As part of the issues in the case, a Florida psychiatrist was sued personally for damages for maintaining the involuntary hospitalization of Mr. Donaldson. The fact that the courts had ruled affirmatively 30 times on the need for the hospitalization of Mr. Donaldson did not exempt the psychiatrist from liability.

"Especially for psychiatrists working in public settings in which staffing was inadequate for delivering satisfactory treatment, the implications of the Donaldson case were disquieting. The easiest way for public institutions to avoid both professional liability for inadequate treatment, on one hand, and civil liability for deprivation of liberty, on the other hand, was to avoid being responsible for the patient in the first place by discouraging admissions or effecting rapid discharge."

The ruling effectively barred huge numbers of mentally ill Americans from the treatment they needed. Thousands were released from hospitals prematurely; thousands more who ought to have been hospitalized were kept out.

Municipal hospitals took in patients, but as acute-care facilities they were permitted to keep patients against their will no longer than thirty days. After that, they were required to release them or recommend their transfer to a state hospital for longer-term care.

But state hospital authorities, responding to *O'Connor v. Donaldson* and similar rulings, routinely rejected all but the very sickest patients, so that in the late 1970s and early 1980s, Manhattan State Psychiatric Center, for example,

153

turned away about 40 percent of all the patients referred to it by city hospitals.

The reluctance of state hospitals to accept mental patients dramatically increased the burden on the short-term-care city hospitals, where, as City Council President Carol Bellamy put it, "Harried doctors became the equivalent of pit-stop mechanics, forced to medicate and release ever-increasing numbers of chronically ill men and women crowding into emergency rooms."

Although the ill effects became increasingly obvious, the rulings remained in force, and, as Dr. H. Richard Lamb, professor of psychiatry at the University of Southern California School of Medicine, noted in *Hospital and Community Psychiatry* in 1984:

"Despite very valid concerns about the shortcomings and antitherapeutic aspects of state hospitals, it was not appreciated [by many deinstitutionalists and patients' rights advocates] that the state hospitals fulfilled some very crucial functions for the chronically and severely mentally ill. The term 'asylum' was in many ways an appropriate one. . . . Patients can easily get lost in the community as compared to a hospital, where they may have been neglected but at least their whereabouts were known."

One of the halfway houses or group homes that were to have replaced the old asylums might have kept Phyllis, and lost patients like her, off the streets—if the facilities had ever materialized.

But instead of shifting funds from the emptying hospitals into programs designed to aid discharged patients, state mental health departments continued to spend the money in the institutions. In New York, for example, only 20 percent of the mentally ill were being treated in hospitals, but

80 percent of the mental health budget continued to be spent on institutions.

This was not primarily a medical decision but a political one orchestrated in large part by powerful unions seeking to save jobs that would be lost if mental hospitals closed—not only health-care jobs, but those of cooks, electricians, truck drivers, plumbers, secretaries, bookkeepers, janitors, all the workers who keep a hospital running. Voters backed the decision, and not only to protect their jobs. They were afraid.

As Dr. Frank Lipton, director of emergency services at Bellevue Psychiatric Hospital, and Dr. Albert Sabatini, the medical director there, note in the 1984 American Psychiatric Association study, "The stigma, apprehension, and fear associated with mental illness make communities resistant to accepting patients into their midst."

The fear, though deeply rooted, is largely based in myth. Few deinstitutionalized mental patients resemble the terrifying homicidal maniacs of television drama. In fact, properly medicated and with the support of social workers, most are quite capable of caring for themselves and their homes in community settings, where their lives can be more satisfying and less oppressive than in the hospitals.

Still, as Dr. Irene Shifren Levine, of the National Institute of Mental Health, put it in the psychiatric association study, "Many citizens do not oppose the theory of community care for the mentally ill, but when faced with the reality, they often oppose the siting of such facilities near their own business or residence."

Thus, in 1974, when the state attempted to open a community-based center for the mentally ill in Queens, Borough President Donald Manes strongly opposed the plan, warning: "The snakepits are being transferred from the institutions to the neighborhoods." Whenever anyone suggested that a mental health clinic be opened in any community anywhere, demonstrations followed, windows were broken, patients were harassed.

As a result, community-based care for the mentally ill became, as Dr. Leona L. Bachrach, a psychiatric research professor at the University of Maryland School of Medicine, put it, an idea for which "our imagination, our creativity and our pocketbooks have generally . . . not been adequate."

In fact, deinstitutionalization never became more than a tangle of unfulfilled promises, and patients were routinely dumped from hospitals with little more than carfare and a pat on the back.

In 1975, for example, a New York Court of Claims judge found the state liable after a discharged mental patient assaulted a couple on a Queens subway platform. The patient, the judge asserted, was not to blame. He had been discharged from a state hospital and "apparently was simply dropped off at a subway station," where "even a well-adjusted individual would no doubt suffer some anxiety." The judge noted that such careless treatment appeared to be "the standard procedure" at the hospital.

Indeed, studies reveal that between 1979 and 1980, 23 percent of all patients discharged from state mental hospitals in New York were sent to "unknown locations," a euphemism for the streets.

Once on the streets, many of the discharged patients were beyond the reach of treatment. "Asking the patient to 'Return home, take the medication, rest, and come back tomorrow,'" says Dr. Stephen M. Goldfinger, director of outpatient services at San Francisco General Hospital, "is a meaningless intervention when home is an alley and rest is impossible."

In any case, as Dr. Lamb disturbingly notes, "Most mental health professionals are disinclined to treat 'street people' or 'transients.' " And, he adds, "We still have not found a way to help some mental health lawyers and patients' rights advocates see that they have contributed heavily to the problem of homelessness—that the patients' rights to freedom are not synonymous with releasing them to the streets where they cannot take care of themselves, are too disorganized or fearful to avail themselves of what help is available, and are easy prey for every predator."

Without the psychiatric support she needed, Phyllis was ill equipped to fend for herself in a hostile city. Her insanity became more deeply entrenched and her chances of finding a home diminished daily.

Even if she could have coped without psychiatric support, and even if she had known that Social Security had approved her claim—the winter came and went before she discovered that—Phyllis's chances of finding an apartment she could have afforded on her $216 SSI allotment were slim or nonexistent. Between 1976 and 1977, New York City rents rose 23 percent, leaving her totally unable to compete for an apartment on the open market.

Public housing was equally out of reach. The number of people needing low-rent apartments skyrocketed in the 1960s and 1970s and peaked during the recession of 1974 and 1975. By then, the New York City Housing Authority had a waiting list of more than 170,000 families, many of whom were told they would probably have to wait fifteen years or more for an apartment. For the homeless there was a special Catch 22—just to get on the list for an apartment, an applicant had to have an address.

Indeed, government regulations and the realities of the marketplace conspired to make homelessness a near-permanent condition. At welfare, for example, only one office in the entire city, a center in a remote location in lower Manhattan, had been designated to accept applications from those who had no address. People who applied at other centers were rarely informed that it existed; they were simply turned away. And even at the lower Manhattan center, prospective clients were required to provide not only their birth certificates and Social Security cards (which could easily be lost or stolen on the streets) but also written proof of the type of support they had received over the past year—even if there had been none.

With no place to turn, Phyllis invested seventy-five cents and took the subway to Manhattan. It was early spring, 1977. Her brother, who by then had found his niche in Times Square, told me he offered to share the dressing room at the One-Forty Bookstore with her, but she turned him down. "She coulda stayed with me for a while, but she didn't approve of the bookstore, which I could sort of understand," Popeye said. "She just took off on her own. You know, sleepin' in parks and stations and stuff."

Later that year, probably as summer approached—it is not clear from the record in just which month this took place—Phyllis phoned the midtown Manhattan Social Security office and learned that her SSI claim had been approved. The money got her off the streets—at least for a while.

Popeye explained: "She got a room in some hotel on the West Side," he said. "But she didn't stay long. She got throwed out." It was an SRO—a single-room-occupancy hotel—he said, but he couldn't recall its name or what street it was on. "I stayed in the place with her for a while but that was a long time ago. I can't remember where it was exactly. Somewhere in the West 50s."

I checked every single-room-occupancy hotel on the West Side from 48th Street to 59th Street. No one could remember a Phyllis Iannotta. I wasn't surprised. If the Bowery flops are for people who live from day to day, the SROs are for those who live from week to week. It is as if they were designed with anonymity in mind. As one bored desk clerk put it: "I can't remember who comes in and out of this dump from one day to the next, and you expect me to remember that far back? Are you kidding? I try to forget. This here is a home for boozers and losers, crazies and skels."

A New York State Assembly report put it another way. "The typical SRO hotel," it noted, "is a cross section of mental, physical and social pathology."

The SROs are all pretty much the same. A tiny room with the john down the hall, minimal decor: a bed and nightstand, a chest of drawers burned by unattended cigarettes, a battered armchair; an ancient porcelain sink that produces only cold water; walls stained in brown inkblot patterns by leaky pipes; linoleum worn in spots to the floorboards by the migration of numberless feet; a grimy window overlooking a dreary street or the rubble at the bottom of an airshaft. Airless in summer, little or no heat in winter; rats year round. Typical rent in 1977 was $50 a week.

Violence and fear are the currency of the SROs. Rape, robbery, beatings, and even murder are so common that the press generally considers them too "cheap" to be reported.

Yet all over the country state mental health departments, lacking the community homes, halfway houses, or any other form of housing, were paying SRO landlords large sums to take in discharged patients. The operating contracts frequently were hastily drawn, ill supervised, and invited abuse. In 1978, for example, columnist Jack Anderson reported that one Illinois rooming-house operator had received $400,000 to house 180 former mental patients. Anderson wrote: "He managed to keep 46 percent of it as profit. He accomplished this feat by spending only 54 cents a day to feed each patient."

In New York, officials rarely bothered to inspect the rooms to insure they were clean and safe, and former patients were thrust among the other outcasts who called the SROs home: alcoholics, addicts, ex-cons, prostitutes, deserted wives and abused women, the handicapped and the elderly abandoned by their families. By 1977, more than 7,000 chronically mentally ill men and women were living in hotels within a few blocks of one another on the West Side of Manhattan alone.

As bad as the SROs were, they provided the only affordable housing available in the city for many of the nation's single poor. But by the mid-1970s, with the country in the worst housing pinch since the postwar crunch, developers began eyeing the decrepit hotels. They saw dollar signs. People with money to spend were clamoring for apartments. With real estate so scarce—in Manhattan, for example, only 2 percent of rental apartments were available at any given time—even the SROs were at a premium. Converted into luxury co-ops and condominiums, housing for nobodies could become housing for somebodies—and huge profits could be made. But first the nobodies had to be gotten rid of.

Developers called the process "gentrification" and pointed out that it would upgrade neighborhoods by bringing in upper-middle-class tenants who would boost the sagging local economy. As one developer put it, "The co-op people will spend a lot of money in the neighborhood for everything from food to clothes and hardware needs." And they did. Low-profit mom-and-pop stores were replaced by fancy boutiques, fashionable cafés took the place of low-budget coffee shops, trendy ice-cream parlors popped up everywhere. Entire neighborhoods were transformed (some said erased) in a matter of months. Business boomed.

In Manhattan, the Schuyler Arms Hotel, once one of the city's most notorious rat holes, became a condominium where residents rode in a glass-enclosed exterior elevator to apartments that commanded $200,000. The Endicott, an SRO where five people's throats had been slashed in a 1972 murder spree, became a luxury condo where the smallest studio apartment cost $150,000. The Hamilton Hotel, where $10 whores had once plied their trade in the hallways, became the cooperative Paramount, a paean to luxury with cut-glass mirrors, hand-painted ceilings, and a lobby covered with rose-colored suede. The Stratton, the Albion, the Columbia. Each went in its turn.

The profits of gentrification were astronomical, but the cost in human terms was even higher. Before long, nearly all the SROs were gone—and, of course, so were their tenants. Most had no place to go but into the streets. There simply was no housing for the poor.

This was not merely a New York phenomenon. Each

year as many as 2.5 million Americans were being displaced from their homes by rent increases, revitalization, and eviction brought on by gentrification.

But little was done to help them find new homes. As early as 1968, President Johnson declared that over the next ten years the federal government should subsidize 6 million units of low-income housing nationwide. However, by 1978, thanks largely to President Nixon's 1973 housing moratorium and the recession of 1974 and 1975, only 2.7 percent of the 6 million units had been built.

New York City actually contributed to the loss of low-income housing by allowing developers to twist a little-known law that had been originally designed to encourage just the opposite. The so-called J-51 tax-abatement law was enacted in 1955 to subsidize rehabilitation of housing in poor neighborhoods by forgiving developers the taxes on improvements for twelve years. Thus if a building were assessed at, say, $1 million before rehabilitation and $5 million afterward, the owner would pay taxes for twelve years on only $1 million.

For a time, the law accomplished what it was intended to. But by the 1970s it had been subverted into a mechanism for converting unprofitable housing for the poor into extremely profitable housing for the well-to-do.

The tax-abatement law enabled some condo developers to reap incomes as high as 56 percent of gross rents, and touched off a wild land grab that helped slash the number of SRO units available to New York's poor from 50,454 to 19,775 by 1982. Another way of putting that is that, in order for developers to create luxury housing for wealthy New Yorkers, more than 30,000 poor New Yorkers had first to be ejected from their homes.

Perhaps Phyllis was one of them.

Developers referred to these wholesale evictions as "passive relocation." But there was rarely anything passive about them. Tenants were purged from their apartments in what became one of the most savage campaigns against the poor ever mounted in this country with the support of public funds.

The tactics were devastatingly simple.

Because the SROs were considered hotels and not apartment houses, rent-protection laws did not apply to them. Landlords could raise rents on short notice or simply change the payment schedule. Toward the end of the month, say, when welfare tenants and those, like Phyllis, on Social Security could be counted on to be short of cash, the landlord might decide to demand payment daily instead of weekly. When tenants couldn't pay, out they went.

In cold weather, the landlord might turn off heat and hot water and try to freeze his tenants out—clearly illegal, but law enforcement was so haphazard that even when fines were levied fewer than 50 percent were ever collected.

Frequently landlords resorted to sabotaging their own buildings. In one publicized case, an SRO landlord purposely destroyed his boiler, then allowed 130 fire and health violations to accumulate. Some of the eighty-five tenants in the building left, but not all. So he waited for them to go out, changed the locks to their rooms, and nailed the doors shut. That got rid of a few more, but some of the hardier tenants removed the doors from their hinges and reclaimed their rooms. The landlord then hired a man with a gun to patrol the hallways. He told tenants it was for their "protection." The result: all eighty-five tenants were forced from the hotel in less than sixty days. A year later, the building was one of the city's most pestigious condos, with apartments beginning at $200,000.

Such tales became common. But little was done to stop the abuses. In most cases they were too complex to be dealt with on the spot by police, and the housing courts were so backlogged that it could take months to resolve cases, by which time the issues would often be moot. Even when courts did mete out punishment, many landlords were not discouraged. In fact, one managed to garner $1.5 million in citizen-subsidized tax breaks to convert his fifteen buildings into luxury condominiums, despite repeated arrests and convictions for coercion and harassment of tenants.

At the height of the J-51 bonanza in 1982, the city was spending almost three times as much on condominium tax abatements as it was on the entire operation of the Department of Housing Preservation and Development, the agency that was supposed to manage the city's housing stock. Outraged, two of the city's political superpowers, the 240,000-member municipal-employee union and the Catholic Archdiocese of New York, that year joined in demanding a moratorium on the conversion of SROs. Yet Mayor Koch, whose campaign contributors included several big J-51 beneficiaries, waited until 1985 to devise a plan to save the hotels.

The plan offered too little too late. Nearly 115,000 SRO units, about 90 percent of the supply, had been lost since 1970. Nationally, single-room housing for the poor was meeting a similar fate. About 1.2 million units, nearly half the supply, had disappeared in the same period—and hundreds of thousands of Americans had lost their homes.

Government was slow to recognize the problem and slower still to act. As New York State Assemblywoman Elizabeth

Connelly, a Democrat from Staten Island, put it in 1981, dealing with homelessness had become "a turf problem, and nobody wants it."

In Albany, Governor Hugh Carey insisted that the homeless were a city problem—a result of its housing policies, especially J-51. "The basic needs of the 'street people'—food, shelter, bath, clothes—are the responsibility of the social welfare system," a 1981 state memo asserted. "Planning for this group must be initiated by New York City and we urge the appropriate city agency to begin this endeavor." Mayor Koch blamed the state's deinstitutionalization policy. "The state policy of releasing deinstitutionalized patients without adequate support has turned the city's neighborhoods into mental wards and the police into hospital orderlies," he said. "What is needed is a coherent state program."

Of course, both Carey and Koch were right. And each might also have blamed unemployment.

Many Americans never fully recovered from the brutal recession of 1974 and 1975, and even as the nation began to pull out of the economic tailspin in the late 1970s and early 1980s, nearly 7 million Americans remained unemployed; as many as 850,000 of them had given up looking for work altogether, according to the Bureau of Labor Statistics. In New York, where unemployment hit 8.8 percent in 1981, one study showed that one-quarter of the men and women in public shelters had recently lost their jobs.

By 1979, as estimates of the homeless in New York soared over 30,000, attorneys for Legal Aid filed a class-action suit in state Supreme Court charging the city and state with violating the state constitution, the city charter, and various provisions of Social Security and mental hygiene laws by failing to provide shelter for all the men who requested it. The suit cited insufficient supply of lodging vouchers in the face of burgeoning demand, the "dangerous and unhealthy" conditions in the Palace Hotel and other flophouses, and the lack of adequate staff at the Men's Shelter.

Oddly, the city did not contest most of the allegations; it simply argued that the issue did not belong in the courts. The state argued that its constitutional and statutory obligations were being met by existing programs, namely home relief, Medicaid, and SSI.

In August 1981, after months of court battles, the city signed a legal paper agreeing to "provide shelter and board to each homeless man who applies for it." The decree prohibited overcrowding and for the first time set minimal standards for health and safety in a shelter.

Ironically, the agreement specified only men, and the city actually went to court to defend its right not to meet the same standards for women.

Meanwhile, city and state officials continued to squabble over how to care for this new homeless underclass. The state urged the city to establish small shelters scattered in residential communities throughout the five boroughs; the city wanted the state to fund huge institutional shelters with several hundred beds each in remote areas.

Mayor Koch was adamant. In September 1981 he told a reporter: "I will not place these homeless men and women in residential communities and destroy those communities. Some people have the philosophy that I should do that but . . . they don't live next to these community houses that they'd like to have. I have an appreciation for the fact that people who are living decent lives don't want the deranged walking their streets. They're sick. . . . So I'm saying we'll provide the facilities. But open up houses in lower and middle income communities? Never! Over my dead body."

A month later, as the city-state debate reached the level of a yelling match, Koch said that establishing community-based shelters would be "like spreading cancers" throughout the city.

Disgusted, State Assemblyman Alexander Grannis, chairman of the Assembly Housing Committee, begged for compromise. "To date," he lamented, "most of our time has been wasted in trading accusations and assigning blame for the homeless problem."

By that time, informed estimates of the homeless in New York City had climbed over 36,000. Koch scoffed, "Thirty-six thousand? No way." He angrily threatened to spend $100,000 just for a head count, then arbitrarily set the figure at "about 12,000." But, he added, "If they are out there and they come to us for a bed and there are 36,000 of them, we'll provide 36,000 beds."

The rhetoric was irrelevant. At the time, city shelters had beds for only 1,700 men and forty-seven women.

Barbara,
Florence,
Pat,
Helen,
Adele,
Gwendolyn

The old stone drinking fountain in Madison Square Park bubbles up perhaps an inch of water when you push the small brass button at its base. Kids stretch up on tiptoe and fasten their mouths over the sun-heated nozzle to suck up the warm, metallic-tasting water or stick a finger over the edge of it to send a jet shooting out to soak a friend. Phyllis would have remembered such fountains from Sunset Park when she was a kid.

But in the New York of Phyllis Iannotta in the year 1977, the fountain in Madison Square Park served more practical purposes.

If you get there by dawn on a summer day, you can see the fountain as Phyllis would have seen it when she first wound up dazed and unprepared on the streets of Manhattan.

Perhaps fifteen or twenty men are lined up in front of the fountain waiting their turn to push the little brass button to wash their faces and their bodies and to brush their teeth.

They work quickly and with amazing thoroughness, holding the button with one hand, cupping water in the other and splashing it on their bodies, bathing their feet and their legs to the knee, then reaching inside their pants or up their skirts to clean thighs and genitals. It is impossible to be private about this, but they try as best they can. Sometimes you will see their laundry drying on bushes in the sun. This is their home.

Often, it was Phyllis's home as well. Many nights she came here to sleep on one of the green wooden benches that extend spokelike through the park. She slept in other parks as well, her brother told me: Bryant Park behind the Public Library on 42nd Street, Union Square on 14th Street, Dag Hammarskjold Plaza near the United Nations.

My search for Phyllis's story took me to those places. Sometimes, as she had, I slept there, and even as a man in good health I found them forbidding. Not without reason. One morning I awoke in Madison Square Park to find that the watch had been stolen from my wrist as I slept. I never felt a thing. The skillful flick of a stranger's razor had simply cut through the band.

By 6:30 in the morning, when the sky is at its most lucid, the fountain bathers have finished and most of them have taken off for the breadline at St. Francis of Assisi Church, which has served the poor since the Great Depression.

It is tempting to say that it is here that New York's homeless begin their day. But that is not so, really, because for the homeless the day had no formal beginning or end. For them, days and nights are void of the comfortable regularity that marks most of our lives: breakfast, lunch, dinner; sleep, rise, work, relax, sleep again.

Instead, they lead restless, nomadic lives, eating when food is available, sleeping in fits and starts, moving from place to place or staying in one spot, but never certain where they will be next or when they will be uprooted.

So the homeless do not *begin* their day on the breadline. But it is safe to say that every day hundreds of them receive a meal here after many hours without food or access to food. And it is safe to say, too, that many hours will pass before most are able to eat again.

The breadline is long and impatient. By 7:00 A.M. it extends more than two blocks: men and women pressed tightly against the buildings, their faces cast toward the pavement, waiting to be handed a thin baloney and cheese sandwich and a cup of coffee by a friar in brown robes and sandals.

Few words are exchanged. Everyone is too tired or angry or humiliated for talk. But I managed to make friends there, people who came, sometimes only after many months, to trust me and share with me a portion of their lives. These are their stories. In each of them there is a piece of the Phyllis Iannotta story, for their trials were her trials; she suffered similar humiliations, similar deprivations; what they endured, she endured as well.

Barbara was once an actress . . . a real actress, not just one of the star-struck dreamers you can find all over the city, but a legitimate professional with stage, film, and television credits. She is tiny, almost elfin, and she played little old lady parts long before she was one.

She still has great stage presence, an unfailing sense of

timing, and a voice that would project with ease into the balcony of all but the very largest theaters. She is quick-witted, acerbic, and sometimes very funny.

Her eyes have a hollow, haunted look. Her face, if it had been cut from cloth, would be a rag: soiled and threadbare, but not quite ready to be discarded. Her hands are small and patrician: well-bred hands, veined in blue and covered, incongruously, with the grime of the streets.

When I first met her she had been on the streets for about a year, living sometimes in shelters but more often in doorways or on a bench in Madison Square Park. She was carrying a mandolin. She told me right up front that she didn't know how to play it. "But," she said, "I like the way it looks and it helps me keep time when I sing." And then, in a voice that would crack brass, she began:

> *"Last night our little baby died* [strum].
> *He died committing suicide* [strum].
> *He had spinal meningitis* [strum].
> *He got it just to spite us . . .* [strum]"*.

She made up the verses as she went along, spitting out mad, angry lyrics like an off-key troubador in a Fellini farce. The effect was jarring, as Barbara knew it would be. She hadn't been in the theater all those years for nothing.

Her repertoire includes several tales on the subject of her homelessness. Exactly how it happened remains as much a mystery as her music. But this much of her story is a constant:

Between acting jobs, she sublet her apartment on Central Park West to "a nice young couple" and took off for Miami. While she was there she suffered a "nervous breakdown" and was hospitalized. She does not offer further explanation.

But, she says: "Nobody doubted that I needed to be in a hospital. I *was* very sick. Yes. Mentally ill. But the place they put me. That was no hospital. It was more like a prison. I felt like a common criminal, a convict on a chain gang. It was barbaric. So I did what any *sane* person would do." She laughed and winked impishly. "I escaped. No James Bond stuff. I just got the hell out."

She lived on the streets of Miami for weeks, panhandling until she got enough money for a bus ticket back to New York.

"When I arrived home, I found that the 'nice young couple' "—she bracketed the air with her index fingers to make the quotations marks—"had taken everything—furniture, rugs, everything—and run away, leaving me to deal with the landlord, who hadn't been paid rent the whole time I was in the hospital.

"They seemed like the most wholesome couple in the world. But they were running a"—her voice dropped confidentially—"a prostitution ring right there in *my* apartment." She paused a beat. "I know because I kept getting calls from her satisfied customers!" She winked, then pursed her lips and made a kissing noise. "That's the way the world works, honey. She was the hooker and I got screwed."

She waited for the laugh, then added with conviction: "I intend to remain homeless for a couple more years, at least. I'll never pay rent again. Never. I'm not going to give my money to some landlord who'll get rich burning women and children in the South Bronx." The reference, of course, was to arson, the slumlord's answer to getting blood from stone. "No," Barbara continued, "I'd rather be homeless than part of that system. And anyway, I meet a better class of people in the street."

After she wound up on the streets, broke and crazy, Barbara's friends abandoned her. "People I had known for years—actors, artists, writers, so-called upper-class people—acted as if they didn't know me. I stopped existing for them. Oh, yes. I am able to get some charity from Actors' Equity. But that's it. As for friends . . ." She didn't have to complete the sentence. "At least in the streets," she said, "people accept you for who you are. Or who you've become."

For a time I lost track of Barbara. Then one day I met her at the soup kitchen run by Holy Apostles Church in Chelsea. She did not look well, and when she spoke thoughts flowed from her in hasty incoherence. But she rummaged through her coat pocket and withdrew an envelope with my name on it. "I'd have gotten it to you sooner," she apologized, "but I didn't have the money for a stamp."

She pressed it into my hand. I started to open it, but she stopped me with an upheld palm. "Read it later," she said. "After I've gone." We exchanged a few more words, and then she shuffled off, trailing a gray blanket after her like a sad, orphaned Linus.

I tore open the envelope and pulled out the letter. It was written on scalloped paper decorated at the corners with bouquets of lilies. In a neat, controlled hand Barbara had written:

Dear Brian,
    I spent a week on the streets of Manhattan following

the snow storm last February that I shall never forget.

It was bitter cold and feet-deep in icy water. We were not allowed to sit down anywhere or to step inside a doorway.

The street people had signals about the "hitman" who was targeting us for assassination [she meant the police who keep vagrants on the move, forcing them into the freezing cold]. When you got the signal, you moved *fast* in the opposite direction to save your life.

That was awful, but I guess the most horrible thing to me was the brutality of the *ordinary citizen*. By the end of the week, my feet were so covered with sores I could barely walk. I crawled uptown hugging the walls for support. And not a single human being offered me a helping hand.

Sincerely,
Barbara

Every time I read that letter, I think of what Barbara told me about meeting a better class of people in the streets.

One of the things that makes so many of the homeless extraordinary is the lengths to which they go, the hardships they endure, to maintain their dignity, their sense of self-worth.

Picture this: a woman of about sixty years, neither tall nor short, a little stout, with curly brown hair and a frumpy green dress. She wears no makeup except, perhaps, some powder (she smells faintly of lavender). Several religious medals dangle from a silver chain around her neck. Her shoes have low heels and lace up the front. They are very proper shoes.

That is Florence. Neat, plain, and very, very straight. In fact, Florence looks rather like a bookkeeper, which is what she was until just a few years ago. In those days, she told me, she lived in a modest but comfortable apartment in Bensonhurst. She kept lace doilies on the backs and arms of the chairs. Now she lives on the floor of the ladies' room at Pennsylvania Station with about fifteen other women. She sleeps on the floor of a public bathroom while secretaries from Long Island walk past her, relieve themselves, and walk out as if she weren't there.

Every day Florence leaves the bathroom and walks to church to attend Mass.

Florence's luck in life was never more than adequate, but until recently it did allow her to work regularly and to have an apartment and to put food on the table. Then, in 1982, her boss told her that he no longer needed her.

Florence collected unemployment benefits until they ran out. Then she went on welfare. Work? There were no permanent jobs. Not for a woman her age. But she did register with an agency, which, after a time, began to find her temporary assignments. She saved what little money she could, and after about a year she decided to go off welfare and work as a free-lance bookkeeper. It meant that she would take home even less money, but she accepted this as the price of her independence.

Florence lived that way for nearly a year. Then, she said, "Somebody stole my handbag. Everything I had was in it—my money, my identification, my food stamps. How stupid I was! I just let myself get ripped off."

Florence couldn't make that month's rent payment. Her landlord said he couldn't wait until she got back on her feet. Property values were skyrocketing; there were more profitable tenants to be had. "My bad luck was his good luck," Florence said stoically. She packed a bag and was gone the next night.

"I had a little money that I'd kept pinned inside my dress," Florence told me. "I was able to get a room in a transient hotel for a week. But after that, my money ran out and I had no place to go. No job, no apartment, no place. It was simple. I was homeless."

Florence took up residence on a bench in a park not far from her former apartment. She kept all her possessions in a suitcase and two overstuffed shopping bags. She rarely left her bench because she couldn't carry everything at once and she was afraid that if she abandoned her bags even for a few moments they would be stolen. "I was just too shaken to get up," she remembered. "I was afraid and stunned. I sat there till I was constipated." She laughed, but the laugh was dry.

One day a man approached her. "He was a stranger, and he asked me what I was doing there. I answered him with just one word: homeless." He gave Florence a subway token. "Take this," he told her, "and go to Olivieri Center near Penn Station." He gave her the address in Manhattan. "They'll help you," he said.

That night Florence sorted through her belongings. She transferred a few things to the suitcase. The rest she just left in the shopping bags on the bench in the park in Brooklyn. She was learning to live within her means. In the morning she boarded the F train to Manhattan. She has not been back to Brooklyn since.

The Antonio Olivieri Center on West 30th Street, also known as the Westside Cluster for Women—or, simply, the Cluster—looks like a refugee station in a war zone. It is not a shelter but a drop-in center where women can spend the day, shower, have lunch, and—most important—see a social worker who will help them obtain government benefits.

It is loud and overcrowded with women slumped in chairs and propped against walls. They are surrounded with shopping carts or bags containing their belongings. Some simply curl up on the linoleum floor or sit on the stairs so you have to step around and over them to get to the administrator's office on the second floor. And there, on a mezzanine level, are more women, lying across desktops and huddled in corners.

Some are in their twenties; others could be seventy or older. They are white and black and Hispanic. Some wear rags, other wear costumes fashioned with great ingenuity, even flair, from scraps of cloth, rug remnants, or old blankets. Most dress conventionally in patiently selected thrift-shop ensembles.

There are women here who have been burned out of their homes, evicted by slumlords, or thrown out by their men. Many are mothers and grandmothers. There are alcoholics, drug addicts, former mental patients, and women, like Florence, who are just down on their luck.

They are ex-housewives, ex-teachers, ex-nurses, ex-secretaries, ex-hookers, ex-cons. Everyone is an ex-something, and they are all homeless.

Some of the women receive Social Security retirement or disability benefits; some get widow's pensions; others have no income except from panhandling. Caseworkers try to help them obtain their entitlements and do what they can to make their lives more comfortable. They provide conversation and some recreation, and sometimes even take them on picnics and outings on their own time and at their own expense.

Still, most of the women have the stunned look of refugees: confused, angry, listless. Their voices fill the room with a jumbled, high-pitched cacophony. Outbursts are common: obscenities shouted into the air, shrieks, screams, crying. Often these are simply ignored; the staff, sometimes, seem too overwhelmed to react except in the most extreme circumstances. Laughter is rare.

"When I arrived there," Florence said, "I knew I was homeless. I knew I was in real trouble." She soon grew restless and frustrated and angry, and one day she got into an argument with an employee. In a burst of anger he told her to leave and not come back.

That is how she wound up on the floor of the Penn Station ladies' room. She has been told repeatedly that she *can* go back to the Cluster, that the man had only lost his temper, that he did not mean what he had said. But Florence said she will never go there again. "I can only take so much," she says. There is no use arguing with her. Her mind is made up. And so this little old lady, who goes to Mass every day scented with lavender, returns to sleep on the tile floor of a public toilet. She has given up on the idea of ever having a place of her own.

She goes there each night about ten o'clock hoping she is not too late to secure a place along the wall toward the back of the anteroom, where most of the women prefer to sleep.

Only a handful of women actually stay in the lavatory itself. They make nests of toilet paper in the stalls and sleep curled around the porcelain bowls. They strip down and bathe themselves in the sinks, then stand hunched up under the hot-air hand dryers.

All this is easily visible from the anteroom. Helen, the sweet, half-crazy former Long Island school teacher who lives there and is the de facto housemother, took a liking to me after I began bringing food to the women and let me spend time there, usually very late at night. Once, she defended my right to be there to a cop who had come to toss me out.

The place is home to an odd assortment of women, from very proper ladies like Florence to foul-smelling, lice-infested madwomen. Helen watches over them like a mother hen, scolding them when they litter, welcoming newcomers, and trying to resolve disputes. The room often erupts in violence, but the women have more to fear from the outside than from each other.

One woman told me of a typical encounter:

"It was about one in the morning, and this bunch of girls, hookers probably, came in. They were wearing these tight designer jeans and fancy tops and they started getting abusive. One of them insisted on pissing in the doorway and she made a woman get up so she could. They all thought it was funny. And they kept yelling things like: 'This is a place to take a piss. *People* don't live here, only *scum*.' Things like that. They kicked one woman's bags and screamed at her. When they left they all said 'Good night, ladies' in a very mocking tone of voice. We have to put up with stuff like that almost every night."

There is no one to turn to for help. Especially not the police. The police, generally, are the enemy of the homeless. They have little use for the "skels" and "maggots," male or female.

The rousts begin at about 2:00 A.M.

Three cops march downstairs to the ladies' room, banging their clubs on the granite walls. The sound echoes like machine-gun fire. Women jump up from their sleep and begin frantically gathering their belongings. But it is too late. The cops block the entrance.

Their voices carry through the station's lower level. "All right, all of you up against the wall," one of them orders. "Line up. Come on, let's go." While one of them calls out a cadence, the women are marched single file upstairs, through the waiting room, and out one of the doors.

Many nights Florence would wander the streets for hours after the police kicked her out of the station. One night after she had been thrown out she said, "You know, I used to believe the policeman was your friend; I used to believe in the Easter bunny, too. Don't ever trust a cop. Now I know why they call them pigs. They don't know anything about justice."

On the streets the women have their own brand of justice. And sometimes it is harsh, too.

"I have found it easier to love than to hate," Pat told me. "But boy oh boy oh boy, I have absorbed so many stabs in the back, so many insults, that I run out of love and my whole body vibrates with hate, so that when I walk down the street people are afraid of me."

Pat's body was as taut as a spring, and as she spoke she thrust her fist into the palm of her hand. A Jew-turned-Muslim, she sometimes uses the name Rahima 37X. She is a former junkie, a recovering alcoholic, and an ex-convict. She's been on the streets since 1956 and she is no more than forty years old.

When I first met Pat she was living in a Hooverville in the meat-packing district near the docks in the West Village. Her bed was a discarded wooden freight pallet on a loading bay.

"Oh, I been in the shelters," she said. "I went one time to the Brooklyn shelter. I came out with body lice and head lice. That was in 1981. In 1983 I went to the shelter in Flushing. I wake up in the middle of the night and there's this bunch of young chicks drinkin' beer and smokin' reefer and makin' a racket. Did anybody stop them? Hah! Then in the morning when I went to take a shower, the bathroom was an abomination to the human race.

"You could say I should be grateful for whatever there is. Beggars can't be choosy. That's so. You're talkin' to somebody who knows the truth of that. But this much is also true. It's the poor workin' stiff who's gettin' stiffed." She smiled at her play on words.

"People go to work. They bust their ass. Take some guy who pushes a truck in the garment center. He makes minimum wage. The government takes money from him. Taxes. They take that money and they piss it away on shelters that are not fit for a dog. And that poor sonofabitch who's tryin' to get by, to feed himself and maybe a coupla kids on his fuckin' minimum wage, you'll excuse my language, is gettin' screwed. Not to mention me. At least on the street you get some respect."

Pat nodded in the direction of a group of white-haired black men around a fire that blazed in an old oil drum on the loading bay. It was night and the fire cast eerie shadows on their faces. "They are the elders," she said. "They worked most of their lives but they never made any money, and when they couldn't work anymore they wound up on the streets. They are good men and they get respect without demanding it. They tend the fire; we get the wood. It gets cold as a witch's tit here at night. If you let the fire go out, you freeze."

There were about ten people living in the camp. Pat was the only woman. They survived on meat scraps left by the butchers and on whatever else they could scrounge.

"At first none of these guys wanted me to do anything because I'm a woman," Pat said. "But I wouldn't have any of that. You let people treat you like that and then they want something in return. I'm my own person. My life and my body are my own. I get wood, I get water from the fireplug, I pull my share. You get nothing for nothing in this world, I always say, and you have to earn your place in heaven."

One of the old men tossed a two-by-four into the drum and the fire popped and crackled. Flames licked up the board, revealing several men sleeping under piles of rags on the loading bay.

Pat continued, her voice rising and falling like a tent evangelist's. "I've been drunk on wine till I'm reelin'. Ooooh yes! Many a time. And I've used every drug imaginable. Lord, I've been everything you could think to call me but a child of God. So it don't matter what *anybody* calls me. I been called it all. But if I can't look you in the eye, brother, I don't want to know you."

Her own eyes are riveting. Set deep in their sockets, they are disconcertingly blue and seem out of place on a face burnished and creased by nearly three decades on the streets. Her hands, which mark time with her words, are deep-veined and scarred with needle tracks.

Pat is proud of her scars. Each one has a story. She pulled up a pants leg. "See that?" she said, showing off an ugly four-inch gash. "I got that from a jive-ass pimp. It

182

was like this. One of my friends had this little dog, and we all went hungry so the little mutt would have something to eat. We loved that little dog. Believe me. Lord, we loved it.

"Well, one day this sonofabitch of a pimp just upped and took that dog away from my friend. I can still hear him laughing. He said *he'd* decide who loved who around here. Well, that just didn't set so good with me, so I goes up to him and I tells him to give the goddamned dog back. He didn't say a word. Not a goddamned word. He just hit me across the leg with a tire iron. God, I can still feel the pain. Broke it bad, he did.

"Well, don't you know the next day they found that pimp lyin' in the street like a dog with a cut halfway across his belly. Of course, he was still breathin', just a little. Now, I wonder who would have done a thing like that? Funny thing. Now we both have scars, that jive-ass bastard and me." She poked her finger at me and nodded sagely. "Respect and justice. That's the way of the streets, my friend. Respect and justice."

Love, certainly, is an almost nonexistent commodity. People find it where and how they can, and then they cling to it.

Helen lives with a dozen cats in an abandoned building on the Lower East Side.

"I'd rather live with a cat than a man any day," she said in her flat midwestern accent. "They're more trustworthy." In fact, it is largely because of her bad relationships with men and her good relationships with cats that Helen has been without a home since 1978.

That was the year her boyfriend took all her money and

kicked her out of the apartment they shared on the Lower East Side. It wasn't much of a place, just two dingy rooms on the fourth floor of a five-story walkup on East 9th Street. The view from her window was of burned-out buildings and winos sleeping in doorways. "The building smelled," Helen said. "The whole building smelled sour. I never got used to it."

Helen tried to make the place nice. She sewed curtains for the windows and made slipcovers from old sheets to hide the holes in the furniture. She had known much better, but this was the best she could afford on her salary as a waitress at Bickford's. "They're not big tippers at Bickford's," she said with humorless understatement.

"It was really *my* apartment," Helen said, folding her arms defensively. "I was there first and I paid the rent. It took everything I had, but I did it. But he convinced me to put the lease in his name, and then when he got tired of me it was good-bye Helen. He actually threw me out. I mean physically. Out of my own apartment. I cried and cried and cried. But I knew what to do. Oh yes. I did not lose my head. There were these people I knew living in an abandoned building down the block. You'd see them all the time. I'd say hello and they seemed like nice people, so when this happened I went to them and asked if I could live there and they said yes."

And so it was that Helen came to live in a room with no heat, no electricity, no water.

"I'm a misfit, I guess. I could have been an engineer. Really. That's what I was studying in college. But things just didn't work out and here I am." She spoke the words softly and without emotion, but she flogged herself with them. Helen has plenty of love for her cats, but very little for herself. "I'm a failure," she told me matter-of-factly. "There's really no other word for it."

Cats curled around her legs and lounged in her lap as we spoke. There were at least five of them, and the sharp smell of their urine mingled with the dampness in the room. Helen cuddled one of them and scratched it behind the ear. A missing chunk of plaster the size of a platter exposed dirty strips of lath in the ceiling and the paint was peeled in layers from the walls—white over blue over pink.

We sat cross-legged on three cushions from an old couch; at night this becomes Helen's bed. An assortment of plastic milk crates serves as tables and chairs and shelves for a jumble of pots and pans and an old two-burner Sterno stove. Candles provide the only light at night. Every day Helen fills two plastic jugs from the fire hydrant and lugs them upstairs for cooking, drinking, and washing up. To use the toilet, she walks two blocks to the tough Puerto Rican bars on Avenue A. She showers once a week at the public baths at Allen Street half a mile away. "I am very careful about lice," she said. "It is very easy to get lice living like this."

Helen was not raised to live this way. When she was a small girl, she lived with her widowed mother, who ran a hotel in a small town outside Chicago. "I had a pretty normal upbringing," she told me. "We lived in the hotel and I helped out. I went away to a private school when I was thirteen. My life was pretty much like anybody else's. The usual ups and downs, highs and lows.

"I went to college for a year. That just didn't work out. I wanted to be an engineer, and my grades were good but I had problems with boys. I've always been a failure in that department. I was involved with this boy and it got, well, serious. At least I was serious. Anyway, that was back in the 1950s, when things were different." She stroked the cat on her lap and struggled for words. Finally, she said, "Lets just say I had a love affair that didn't work out and I needed a change, so I dropped out.

"I worked in offices for about seven years. I was bored a lot and I didn't relate well to the other secretaries. I was better educated and had different interests, but I just couldn't get motivated to do anything else. Remember, too, there weren't as many opportunities for women then as there are now."

Helen looks like a child of the 1950s. Her face is as freckled as a *Saturday Evening Post* teenager's and she still wears her light brown hair in a pert ponytail that sways as she walks. Although her ill-fitting polyester church-basement hand-me-downs betray a middle-aged bulge, it is not hard to imagine her slim and wearing a pullover sweater and a gray flannel skirt with saddle shoes.

"Men found me attractive," she said in her matter-of-fact way. "I could never understand it. I never thought of myself as pretty. But men, well, I don't know how to say this. They always came on to me. I was interested, but I didn't know what to do, what to say. I wasn't exactly shy. It's just that I didn't have any self-confidence. I think men thought I was stuck up."

Then, one night as she was coming home from work, a man got off the elevator with her and followed her to her door. As she fumbled in her bag for the key, he calmly produced a knife and invited himself inside. Helen remembers very little about the man except that he was white and had hairy hands. One hand held the knife. The other forced its way across her body and struck at her when she resisted. When he left there was blood smeared across her legs.

"I told my mother what happened," Helen said. "But she was a cold, unfeeling person. She said if anything like that ever happened again, I'd better not bother coming home. I had a complete nervous breakdown after that. I just fell apart. I tried to handle it on my own. I didn't even go to a doctor. But I couldn't ever live in that place again. I had to get out of the building, out of Chicago, away from my mother, away from everything."

So she took the Greyhound cure. She arrived in New York with only a few hundred dollars in savings and no friends. But she quickly found a low-rent apartment on East 4th Street and a job as a waitress in an East Village café. For a time it seemed that all she had needed was a change of scene. But she continued to be haunted by fears of the man with the knife.

"I didn't have any friends, and I was getting more and more disturbed. I had no one else to turn to, so I went to a psychiatrist. I thought maybe it would help, but he wasn't right for me. I didn't get any better, I just went broke paying him. Maybe if I'd had good psychiatric treatment things would have turned out differently. Who knows?"

As it was, Helen simply slipped deeper and deeper into depression. "I could never learn to hate men," she says. "I wish I could have, maybe it would have helped take away the hurt. But mostly when I saw a man, I just wanted to be loved, to be held, to be comforted. That's not so strange, is it?"

Then, on a spring morning in 1966 she was raped again, this time by a man who climbed in a window from the fire escape. "After that I had another nervous breakdown," Helen said. Her voice was a monotone, devoid of emotion.

After this second attack, Helen stopped going to work

and went on welfare. She moved out of her apartment on East 4th Street—"I couldn't stand to be there. I could always feel his presence in the room"—and moved in with a family in Brooklyn that let her have a room in exchange for taking care of their two small children. That lasted two years, but when the mother stopped working Helen was out of a job and a home.

After a brief, unsuccessful attempt at living in a hippie commune, Helen found the apartment on East 9th Street. A few months later she met Rick. "He was much younger than me and he wasn't exactly what you'd call handsome, but I really loved him. And he loved me, too, I think. He was interested in the things I had to say. We shared our deepest thoughts and made love, and for about a year everything was wonderful. He worked at odd jobs, did some carpentry, things like that. But he never had any money. I was working at Bickford's at the time and supporting both of us. It took everything I made to keep us alive."

And then Helen stepped on a piece of broken glass on her way to work. It cut through the sole of her tennis shoe and sliced her foot. "It didn't look too bad, so, like a dope, I let it go. My foot got infected. I couldn't work with an infected foot. So there was no more money coming in. We started fighting and then just like that Rick threw me out. Sometimes I wonder how life would have been different if only I'd put some iodine on that cut."

Helen found comfort in the love of a stray cat that adopted her in the abandoned building on East 9th Street. "There we were. A *jilted* woman and a *stray* cat in an *abandoned* building." She emphasized each word, dragging out the irony. "It was perfect."

What she didn't know, she said, was that her cat was pregnant. Soon there were four more cats. "I couldn't bring myself to give them away," Helen said. "They were so cute, and so defenseless. I just couldn't abandon them. I loved them so much." She held up the cat on her lap and touched her nose to its nose and talked to it in baby talk. "You know," she confided, "cats are very loving animals, despite what many people think. They saved my life. I mean that literally.

"That winter," she continued solemnly, "the temperature went down to zero. I went to sleep fully dressed, with my coat and hat and gloves on and still I was cold. But the cats snuggled up with me under the old blankets I had and we kept each other warm. I think if it hadn't been for the cats I would have frozen to death that winter. Truly."

That spring, Helen told me, she decided to go to the Women's Shelter. She was told to go to a newly opened annex in the Bushwick section of Brooklyn. "It was one of the worst experiences of my life," she said. "As soon as you got off the subway around the corner from the shelter, hordes of little boys—I mean grade-school boys, little street urchins—would mob you and try to take your handbag. You had to fight them off. Then at the shelter it was just awful. Terrible. Terrible. Terrible.

"The first night I didn't sleep a wink. There was one woman going around trying to rip off other women while they were sleeping. There was a lot of drinking and some marijuana. There were plenty of staff people, but all they would do is make bed checks. They didn't do anything to break up the drunken parties or to stop the violence. There was no place to put your things, and if you left anything around it would get stolen. So I kept all my belongings in a shopping bag and at night I went to sleep with them under my pillow."

Every day, Helen saved the $1.50 subway money she

received at the shelter and trudged back to Manhattan across the Brooklyn Bridge to the building on East 9th Street, a distance of about seven miles each way. "I had to feed my cats," she said. "I couldn't just let them starve. Not after they saved my life."

Ultimately, she moved back in with them. "I was scared stiff at the shelter. It was much safer to live in an abandoned building. And anyway, here I have my cats. They're all I can count on."

Mostly, the homeless have to count on others for their survival. But this dependency on charity is, even at its best, humiliating, especially for the many women who have reared children and managed families for most of their lives.

"You've got to roll with the punches in this life." Adele said it as if it were her motto. And it could be. She's been punched plenty by life in the past few years. But you'd never know it. Adele looks like your basic polyester-slacks, middle-aged suburban housewife, which is exactly what she was for most of her adult life. I picture her loading groceries from the Seven Eleven into a station wagon.

You would never suspect that she'd spent the last five years of her life on the streets and in shelters, wearing hand-me-downs from strangers and dining in soup kitchens. Adele has never given up on her past nor fully accepted her present. She still refers to the homeless around her as *them* instead of *us*.

When she speaks of her past, her voice goes flat, as if the memory of it is so loaded with emotion that she is deadened by the weight. "We were just an ordinary family," she told me. "Nothing special about us, I guess. Just George and me and our son Albert." She stared off into space for what seemed like a very long time. Then: "We had a nice little place in the Rockaways, nothing much, but we were happy there."

Her husband, she said, was a lineman for Long Island Lighting Company and her son dreamed of becoming a mechanical engineer. "He went to Catholic school and he worked hard," she said of her boy. "He was accepted to Pace University, but he was diabetic and he was only a year there when he died. He just went into shock and died." She held a hand over her eyes. "He wasn't even twenty years old." Then a year later her husband had a heart attack and he died too. "It was just too much, I thought *I* was going to die. Sometimes I wish I had. There I was, forty-six years old, a widow, no job, no money in the bank, no nothing."

She did receive a widow's pension—$270 a month. But how far could she stretch $9 a day? Adele gave up her apartment and took a furnished room in a run-down hotel. She tried to find work but, as she put it, "Who wants to hire a middle-aged woman with no experience in anything but being a housewife, when they can hire a girl fresh out of high school with no experience in anything but looking sexy?"

Meanwhile, the cost of everything—food, clothing, shelter—continued to climb while her pension remained the same month after month. "Out in the suburbs a woman in my situation stands out like a sore thumb," Adele said. "People would point and say, 'Look at the shopping bag lady.' I just couldn't stand that, so I decided if I was going to be a bag lady—and the plain truth is that I am a bag lady, you know—I decided I would try to be anonymous. So I came to the city."

Since then, Adele has stayed in the municipal shelters

and in church shelters, living with other women who have given up on the idea of ever having a home of their own. "I hate it," she said bitterly. "I hate living on charity. I want to be thankful. I *ought* to be thankful. Without charity I would die. But sometimes it is very hard to be grateful. I can't show any emotion. What choice do I have? When you take charity you have no choices."

That winter Adele had lived with fifteen other women in a makeshift dormitory thrown up in a church basement. "It was very nice," she said, "and the people from the church were very nice, too. But then spring came and that was the end of that."

The church closed the shelter and Adele and the others were transferred to another church basement. Then, two weeks later, that shelter closed. One by one, the churches began closing their shelters. In one month, Adele shifted to four different church basements until, finally, there were none left. "That meant no bed for Adele," she said. "No place to go. So here I am, on the streets. What do they think? That winter is the only time a woman needs a bed?"

Adele might have spoken the words with Gwendolyn in mind.

Gwendolyn is a princess of the streets. She drapes her body with gowns pieced together from old negligees and wears her golden hair in braids wrapped around her head like a crown. Her skin is as white as alabaster, her eyes are the color of aquamarines. She walks as if on air, pirouetting on broken high heels, head held high, waiting for romance and the white knight who never comes.

She has settled for less, of course, for the embraces of strangers who take her home and keep her warm for the night and sometimes give her food or money. But in the morning they always leave her back in the streets. They don't understand. But no matter. She can wait.

When we met, Gwendolyn was living in a former school building in Greenwich Village that had been converted hastily into a temporary shelter by a group calling itself the Caring Community. The large, dusty gymnasium became a dormitory, and under the guidance of a good and patient woman named Susan Williams the place became a home, a place where twenty-three women came together off the streets, broke bread, and shared in each other's lives. It was, in fact, a community of caring. It was a rare place.

To Gwendolyn, that huge old gym must have seemed like a mirrored ballroom, for she waltzed and promenaded and smiled her enigmatic smile. She was always the belle of the ball in her private world. No one minded or told her to stop or to go away. It was a place where Gwendolyn could be Gwendolyn.

Then one day the City of New York, which owned the large red-brick building, shattered Gwendolyn's fantasy. It ordered the shelter closed. The building was to be sold.

The Caring Community sent a letter to the women at the shelter hoping it would arrive before the city marshals did.

"Dear Friends," it began. "We hope the Caring Community shelter has been of some help during the long and bitter winter. Unfortunately, we are faced with eviction by the City of New York and will have to give up this building and the shelter . . . We regret, therefore, that we must close the center Friday, May 6." The letter arrived Thursday, May 5. Susan Williams said it was like "kicking the crutch out from under a cripple."

The night before they all left, someone bought a bottle of cheap champagne and they mixed it with orange juice, making Mimosas to stretch it. There was cake and cookies and everybody tried to turn a wake into a party.

The next morning, one of the women opened her bible to the Book of Lamentations and wrote the words on a large paper banner:

"The thought of pain, my homelessness, is bitter poison. I think of it constantly and my spirit is depressed. Yet hope returns when I remember this one thing: the Lord's unfailing love and mercy still continue, fresh as the morning, as sure as the sunrise. The Lord is all I have, and so in Him I put hope."

They tacked the sign on the old school door and everyone walked out. They closed the door behind them. They joined hands in prayer, and then they walked away into the streets.

The women who lived with Gwendolyn scattered throughout the city. Some went to live in the ladies' room at Penn Station, some chose to go to the Olivieri Center, where they could sleep sitting up in chairs or on the floor—in violation of health and fire regulations. None went to the Women's Shelter. They all had been there at one time or another, and they refused to endure it again.

Gwendolyn simply moved to a park bench about 100 feet from the locked entrance of the school. She liked the neighborhood, she said.

The other women worried about Gwendolyn alone on the bench. They knew what Gwendolyn refused to admit. She was pregnant. They begged local churches to take her in. They explained why they were so concerned. But no one offered Gwendolyn any other place to live.

Two weeks after the shelter in the brick schoolhouse

closed, on a rainy night, Gwendolyn gave birth on the bench outside the locked building where she had once lived. Two cops driving by stopped, helped with the delivery, and took Gwendolyn to St. Vincent's Hospital a block away.

Miraculously, the baby was healthy and cheerful. When I visited them in the hospital Gwendolyn told me she had named the baby Barbara Nancy, after one of the women she lived with in the building at 13th Street. She also said she had decided to give the baby up for adoption.

She did not know who the father was; he was not the white knight.

The
Dwelling
Place

Sister Nancy Chiarello was wearing the same blue plaid shirt and overalls she had on the day Phyllis's body was found. But this time the dark mourning lines were gone from under her eyes and she was smiling.

As we climbed the steep stairs to the second floor of the Dwelling Place, the banging pots and pans and the shuffle of chairs announced the evening meal as surely as any dinner bell.

The stocky young nun ushered me into the dining room. "This is Brian," she announced. "He's come to be a volunteer. I hope you'll all make him welcome." Old women, toothless hags dressed in rags, and attractive young women barely out of their teens sat expectantly at tables covered with blue-checked oilcloth as volunteers passed them plates heaped high with tuna and macaroni casserole.

I worried that they would resent my intrusion, that they would peg me as a kind of voyeur, which, in a sense, I was.

Some of them looked up from their plates. Others ignored me and continued to eat. No one said anything to acknowledge my presence.

Sister Nancy pulled a chair out from the table. "Sit down," she said. "I'll get you something to eat, then we'll get you started." She sat me next to an old black woman wearing a blue baseball cap festooned with colored scarfs and placed a plate of macaroni and a cup of coffee in front of me. "Buon appetito," she said. She placed a hand on my shoulder and squeezed. "Don't worry," she laughed, "Grace here won't bite you." Grace looked at me and smiled a snaggle-toothed smile, then attacked her macaroni.

The ladies ate hungrily but slowly, savoring each mouthful. No one said a word to me until I was finished eating. Then Grace turned to me. "Well," she said, "it looks like we survived dinner. Would you be so kind as to get me a cup of coffee? I take it light with five sugars."

"Five sugars?"

"Five sugars, honey. How do you think I stay so sweet?" She threw her head back and laughed. I had made a friend among the ladies of the Dwelling Place.

As a volunteer, I worked at the Dwelling Place from 6:00 P.M. to about midnight every Friday. I served food and washed dishes and mopped floors and heaved heavy cans of garbage. I mediated disputes, listened to long stories—some sad for the truth in them, others for their measure of delusion—and traded bad jokes for good laughter. I had come to learn about Phyllis Iannotta and the life she had led here. I wound up learning a lot about myself as well.

Every week Nickel Louise would greet me at the door with a cheerful "Hi, Little Papa. You heard any good news?" And every week I'd tell Louise that in my line of work good news was bad news, and we'd laugh. Louise got her name from her habit of leaving a nickel in the doorways she used to sleep in. When I met her, she had been off the streets for about two years and was living on a chair under the stairs at the entrance to the Dwelling Place.

Louise rarely mixed with the other ladies. She was too busy with her pregnancy (Louise had been pregnant for about two years; the baby was due any day now) and her plans for a trip to North Carolina ("Got everything packed and ready to go, soon's I have this baby"). The Dwelling Place had saved Louise from the streets. For some time, she had been giving her nickels to Sister Nancy.

The Dwelling Place has saved hundreds of homeless women from the streets. More than a score of volunteers and nearly half that many nuns have come and gone since it opened. By the time I arrived, there were four nuns living at the house on West 40th Street—sisters Nancy, Mary, Jackie, and Naureen. Only Sister Nancy had been there from the beginning.

The idea for the Dwelling Place began with the view from a tenement window. It was March 1977, Sister Nancy recalled, and she was leaning on the windowsill of the tired apartment where she was living on West 47th Street. Outside, an old woman dressed in rags hunched down over the garbage can at the curb. She was pulling out bits of food, remnants of a meal Sister Nancy and her roommates had eaten—had said grace over—only hours before. The young nun recoiled as the old woman put a scrap of bread into her mouth and began to chew slowly. "It reminded me of what St. Francis said," she told me, and she recited:

"When I was in sin, it appeared too bitter to me to see lepers; and the Lord himself led me among them, and that which seemed bitter to me was changed for me to sweetness of soul and body."

That night she told her roommates what she had seen. Like Sister Nancy, Regina Cassanto and Bernadette Mullen were Franciscan Sisters of Allegeny and nurses at St. Clare's Hospital at 51st Street and Ninth Avenue. They had come together through their common faith, their desire to live communally, and their devotion to the poor. Their mentor was Francis of Assisi.

"We were living pretty frugally," Sister Nancy told me one night, "but still we knew we were not living in solidarity with the poor. We wanted very much to live as we felt we should. We took one look around us—the furniture, the refrigerator stocked with food, all of it—and we said to ourselves, we're not even coming close."

A dream began to take shape: they would find a building, it did not have to be large, and they would shelter homeless women there and feed them. They would live with them, too. For this place, they told themselves, would be a home, not an institution.

"We had no idea of how to go about things," Sister Nancy said. "And so every night after work we went out and canvassed the neighborhood, looking for buildings and meeting with the ladies in the streets—getting to know them, letting them get to know us, and sharing our dream with them. We wanted it to be their dream, too."

All three nuns were working in demanding jobs: Nancy in the gynecology clinic, Bernadette in the intensive-care unit, Regina as a private-duty nurse caring for a cancer patient.

"We each took a block a night," Sister Nancy said. "All spring we looked at abandoned buildings, at old warehouses and factory buildings. Sometimes a building would look good, but for one reason or another it wouldn't be right. Too big, maybe, or too small or too dilapidated or out of our price range—which, of course, was really zero because we didn't have any money. Our order said they weren't supporting any more experimental communities. But we knew the money end would take care of itself."

That summer, after months of looking, the nuns found their building. It was a dilapidated five-story tenement on West 40th Street, just around the corner from the Port Authority Bus Terminal. It was occupied by a drug rehabilitation program that was seeking release from its lease. And, by happy coincidence, the landlord was the Catholic Archdiocese of New York.

But when the nuns approached bishops at Archdiocese headquarters, they were told the house was part of a valuable three-building real estate package that couldn't be broken up. In desperation, they decided to appeal directly to Terrence Cardinal Cooke, the aloof archbishop of New York. "We just walked uptown to the cardinal's mansion and knocked on the door," Sister Nancy laughed. "We didn't know anything about protocol, but we were about to get a lesson."

They were told that His Eminence was on retreat, that they would have to make an appointment. Instead, the nuns came back with a quickly scrawled note and slipped it to the cardinal's maid. "Please," they pleaded, "put this under his pillow."

200

Sister Nancy recited it from memory: "We beg you as shepherd of the flock of New York not to sell the building on West 40th Street. It is an ideal building for homeless women."

Not long afterward, the nuns were informed the building would not be sold, that they would be allowed to convert it to a shelter. "Our prayers had been answered," Sister Nancy said. "We were overjoyed."

A few weeks later, the priests of St. Francis of Assisi Church on West 31st Street—the breadline church—offered a special Mass for the new shelter. The priests understood the nuns' dream better than most. After the service, many communicants gave the nuns money for their project. A young man named John Dowdell offered them something far more valuable—commitment. Dowdell was a member of Dignity, a group of homosexual Catholics dedicated to community service. We met at the church one morning after Mass. "I thought the nuns had a wonderful, inspiring idea," Dowdell told me. "And I saw that we might be of service." The following week, he produced fifteen men eager to help the nuns set up the shelter: to wield hammers and shovels and do dirty work and heavy lifting.

Some of them had required convincing.

"Shopping bag ladies? Bugs? Lice? Disease? Oh no, that wasn't for me. I just wanted a good time," Dignity volunteer Rodney Muhlon told me one night at the Dwelling Place. "Oh, my, they had to do some talking to get me involved. But eventually I realized that this was an important thing, not so much for the ladies as for us. Gay people are oppressed and the ladies were oppressed. We understood each other. There was no such thing as a faggot to them. They accepted us as human beings; we accepted them as human beings. We cared about each other. That sounds simple enough. But do you realize what a rare thing that is? So anyway, I volunteered. And then I worked my buns off."

Work began at once.

"The building was a wreck," Muhlon recalled. "So we just started at the top and shoveled the dirt and debris down as we went. We all pitched in and cleaned and painted and made repairs. It was hard work, but it was good work. We joked around, acted crazy, and had a ball. And the nuns were just as crazy as we were. We called them the 'lovable nitwits.' "

Meanwhile, others were scrounging: for clothing, for pots and pans and tableware, for lumber and nails and paint, for beds and bedding and furniture. Everything was accomplished on a shoestring and a prayer. Especially prayer.

"There were any number of little miracles," Muhlon remembered. "The nuns would go upstairs and pray, and people would come knocking at the door. Take the time we really needed a carpenter. We couldn't do the work ourselves, but who had the money for a carpenter? So we prayed." He laughed. "Can't hurt, right?"

"Well, lo and behold, two hours later a woman comes to the door. She says, 'I'm a carpenter. Do you need a carpenter?' So she comes in with her toolbox and she goes right to work. She puts down her level and very seriously looks at one of the guys and says, 'Nothing in this damn house is straight.' She was in a building full of gay people and she couldn't understand why everybody was laughing!

"Another time, we needed paint, lots of paint. Our prayers were answered. We got a donation. Rose beige. Gallons of it. We painted the whole damn house rose beige. Sister Nancy hated the color and she'd joke that it was a gift from the devil—and it was. We got it all free from the Red Devil Paint Company. That's what it was like. A lot of prayers answered, a lot of laughter, a lot of very wonderful times."

Throughout the summer, everyone referred to the developing shelter simply as "The House," until one day the nuns received a letter from their former provincial, an older, much-loved nun who praised the project and wrote: "I wish you God's blessing in your new dwelling place."

The phrase struck a chord from the Book of Psalms. "How lovely is thy dwelling place," the verse says, ". . . even the sparrow finds a home." The name stuck.

The Dwelling Place opened its doors on October 4, 1977—the Feast of St. Francis. On the walls of every floor, hand-lettered banners spelled out the nuns' simple philosophy: "Love and Never Count the Cost," "It Is When You Give of Yourself That You Truly Give," "Be Always Little, Simple, Poor." The Dwelling Place would restore the muscle to those clichés.

On the first floor was a laundry room and a clothing room where the ladies could select their wardrobes from an array of hand-me-downs. (Here Nickel Louise obtained the wide men's ties she habitually wore, and Red Rooster, a demented alcoholic streetwalker, once found a gold lamé cocktail dress to strut her stuff in, such as it was.)

The heart of the house was on the second floor with its large living room where ladies could lounge in chairs and watch TV or play an old not-quite-in-tune upright piano. Here too was the dining room and the kitchen, where huge pots of soup or stew simmered perpetually on the stove, infusing the whole house with the smell of home.

The third and fourth floors were dormitories, and on the top floor was the small chapel.

There were twenty-four beds, and that first night the nuns worried that more women might come than there were places to put them. Instead, only one woman showed up.

Ida arrived toting four shopping bags, two in each hand, and smelling like a damp cellar. She was hunched over from years of carrying her preposterous bundles and looked, as Rodney Muhlon put it, "slightly in need of a shave." She stood at the door grinning a toothless grin, like a witch who had just heard a good joke, and then walked in as if she owned the place, which in a sense she did.

No one knows just how Ida found out about the Dwelling Place—the nuns had never met her on their nightly forays into the streets—but it was clear she had come to stay. "All the poor woman wanted was a little sleep," Sister Nancy said. "But we just kept fussing over her, waiting on her hand and foot. She was a real celebrity that night."

The next night four more women showed up. But by the end of the week, word had gotten out. All twenty-four beds were filled and others who came were asked to sleep in chairs. Within two weeks, as many as sixty women a night were sleeping shoulder to shoulder on cots, in chairs, and on mats on the floor in every room of the little building.

Pockets was among the first to arrive. She had been a denizen of the streets for two decades or more. For many years, she had perched in a huge concrete planter in front of the Holland Hotel on 42nd Street, a few blocks from the Dwelling Place.

You couldn't miss her, for even in the hottest weather Pockets wore three, sometimes four, brightly colored sweaters and layer after layer of loudly clashing skirts. Into each skirt she sewed many pockets, and into the pockets she put everything she owned and much that she did not own. Pockets had a habit of liberating things from their rightful owners. The practice defined her personality and gave her her name.

At the Dwelling Place, Pockets rarely left the security of a tiny bench in the downstairs hallway. But from time to time she dashed up the narrow staircase to the kitchen in a wild foray for food. Ann Quintano, a former live-in volunteer who had been on the streets for a time herself, remembered the kitchen chaos Pockets could create:

"She would race upstairs like a bat out of hell, darting from the sugar bowl to the tea urn to the bread box, grabbing everything in huge quantities and stuffing them into her pockets.

"She would snatch anything she could get her hands on and people would be blocking her route here and there and trying to direct her downstairs, and she would be shouting or talking, not quite so you could understand her. Nothing you could say would stop her. She wasn't going to listen to anybody right then. She felt she was well within her rights to take what she wanted and she was getting what she was getting."

Sometimes one of the nuns would tell Pockets that if she did not give back what she had taken she would have to leave. But Pockets would have none of that. She owned the Dwelling Place, after all, and given the slightest provocation, she would pull out a sheath of legal papers, ripped from the libers at the Hall of Records, fan them out like a deck of cards, and shout, "I have the deeds to this goddamned place and nobody can tell me what to do."

Then there was Gloria. Tiny and plain, with a body shaped

like a potato and skin as pale, she was addicted to soap operas, perhaps because her life had been so much like one. Before she came to live at the Dwelling Place she had been living with a junkie who took over her apartment, stole her money, then threw her out and brought in another, prettier, girl.

Gloria was made to be used. Slightly retarded, she wanted nothing more than to please. She used to cop drugs for her boyfriend and, although she is painfully innocent, sometimes even turned tricks for the money to support his habit. She was crushed when he threw her out, and she spent long weeks just sitting on a bench in the Port Authority Bus Terminal staring into space before the nuns found her and convinced her to come to the house on West 40th Street.

There, perhaps for the first time in her life, Gloria met people who loved her without abusing her first. Still eager to please, she helped with the cooking, the cleaning, and the laundry, and soon she was taking new arrivals under her wing, showing them the ropes, and, every afternoon without fail, drawing them into the living room to watch "As the World Turns."

Gloria bustled around the place all day in her housecoat with her short, dark hair in curlers and her nose into everything. To her the Dwelling Place was a home, and she was the housemother.

As outgoing as Gloria was, Charlotte was withdrawn. Charlotte had hit bottom. She was an alcoholic, a heavy drug user, and a Hell's Kitchen whore, which is to say she was a hooker of very last resort. She came to the Dwelling Place infested with lice and, it was thought, infected with syphilis. Her clothes were filthy and she stank. She was no more than thirty-three years old.

When she arrived, she talked to no one and slept sitting up on the bench in the entranceway. No one knew her full name, and for months everyone referred to her as Charlotte Downstairs. They took meals to her downstairs and left her, as they thought she wanted to be, alone.

But there are few people who want to be left alone completely. More often, they simply want to be accepted on their own terms.

When Charlotte realized that there were no strings attached to her staying at the Dwelling Place, she began, slowly, tentatively, to come out of her shell. Of her own accord she began to bathe; she requested clean clothes. She moved upstairs, and began to help prepare meals; she took an interest in the other ladies. She asked for help in getting financial assistance, and after much wrangling Social Security granted her SSI benefits. Eventually, she moved into a residence hotel and started a new life.

The process—although it was not a process at all, since there was nothing clever or preconceived about it—took months. But there was no hurry. There was nothing efficient about the Dwelling Place. Nuns, volunteers, the ladies—all bustled about preparing and serving meals, washing dishes, doing laundry, sorting clothing donations, delousing, rushing with mop and bucket to battle perpetually problematic plumbing, salving leg ulcers, watering houseplants, fighting bureaucratic paper wars, arbitrating squabbles.

"Everything was always in a state of controlled chaos," Ann Quintano recalled. "It was wonderful. Everything would be going on at once and then, out of the blue, Sister Perry might show up and it would be party time. Just like that."

Elna Lee Perry, a self-anointed minister of the Lord, is a Times Square fixture with her autoharp and her unique

207

brand of old-time religion. Pushing seventy, Sister Perry says (to anyone and everyone), "I gave myself to the Lord when I was six years old. I had white folks' hair back then and it was straight as could be and long down to here. Now I'm a child of God and ever'thing about me is natural."

There were innumerable excuses for parties at the Dwelling Place. "Oh," said Gloria, "we do know how to have a good time. We sure do."

There was only one alternative to the Dwelling Place back then, the forty-seven-bed Women's Shelter on Lafayette Street on the Lower East Side. Having a good time was not one of its precepts, but it certainly was efficient.

The women there, referred to as "clients," were required to surrender all their money and to open their bags for inspection as a condition of admission.

Then came what shelter workers called "intake," but which was more like an interrogation by a bored aide with a blank form in front of her. Name? Social Security number? Last address? Why did you leave there? Next of kin? Have you ever been hospitalized for mental illness?

To the homeless, who live in a world where every aspect of life is conducted literally out in the open, privacy is a rare, treasured commodity. On the streets, no one asks for names. It is an unspoken rule, a matter of common courtesy. This is not unreasonable. Many among the homeless are running from something: from their families, from abusive men, from immigration authorities. To surrender a name is to assume a risk.

To some, like Ellen, the jeopardy exists in a bizarre dimension.

"I can't tell you my name," she once told me. "They'll

get you if I do. It's not worth the risk." She was convinced that if I knew too much about her, devils—to her very real demons, like something from Hieronymus Bosch—would find me and torture me until I revealed her whereabouts. Then we both would be lost. She believed this as absolute truth. She did not care to discuss it, to explain it, or to make it seem rational.

Ellen was living in Penn Station because she had been denied a bed at the Women's Shelter for refusing to disclose her name.

Revealing her name was the least of the invasions a woman had to endure for a bed at the Women's Shelter. After the "intake," each woman was led down a corridor without explanation, handed a cup of foul-smelling "shampoo" to kill lice, and ordered to take a shower. Finally she was forced to submit—of all things!—to a gynecological exam.

Mealtimes at the Women's Shelter had nothing of the cheerful informality of the Dwelling Place, where food was cooked from scratch—often by the ladies themselves—and served family-style on brightly covered tables.

At the Women's Shelter, meals, though nutritional, were bleak, bland, soggy, overcooked, and institutional. Second helpings were unheard of.

Attendants assigned women their seats at the dinner table, denying their requests to sit with friends. One day when I visited, orders and announcements—"Sarah Jones report to the office," "Alice Wilson you have a telephone call"—were blared over a loudspeaker throughout the meal, and the air was thick with racial animosity and homosexual innuendo. Women ate their meals hurriedly. They avoided each other and seemed to talk no more than was necessary.

At night, "clients" told me, curfews were strictly enforced, and mornings were met with soldierly regularity: wake-up was at 6:30 A.M.; beds were to be made with hospital corners and kept tight as drums. Although many were kept awake during the night by hourly bed checks, the women were not permitted even to lie on top of their beds until after the evening meal.

All in all, the Women's Shelter was a loud, frightening, restrictive, intrusive, and generally unpleasant place to be. A review of their records shows that Phyllis Iannotta never stayed there.

Perhaps she was one of those turned away from the shelter in 1977 for lack of beds. Perhaps she was one of the 350 rejected that year for failure to comply with the rules. Perhaps she never applied. The cold regimentation of the Women's Shelter and the intrusive admission procedures—especially the mystifying requirement for a GYN exam—kept hundreds of women away.

Contrary to popular mythology, they did not refuse shelter because they preferred life on the streets. "It would be more accurate," a study by the Manhattan Bowery Corporation pointed out in 1979, "to say that these women resist excessive handling, rules and regulations which they find intrusive, and like many older women, they cling to what is familiar for a sense of security, even if familiarity takes the form of a few overstuffed shopping bags."

And even the most disturbed go out of their way to make homes for themselves.

Kai had lived for perhaps five years in a house she built of orange crates and cardboard cartons at 41st Street and Ninth Avenue across the street from the Port Authority Bus Terminal. She placed her tiny hut against the wall of the old, vacant Lamston's five-and-ten, the same building behind which Phyllis Iannotta's corpse was found. Years before, Kai had worked there as a countergirl, serving hot dogs and wedges of lemon meringue pie. She lost her job when Lamston's closed. But she kept coming back, until, at last, she decided to make her home there.

She built her house with painstaking attention to detail. First she laid wooden orange crates out to form a simple but durable foundation. Then up went walls of cardboard cartons, forming a four-foot-high barricade that she roofed over with discarded pieces of carpeting and oilcloth held down at the corners with stones.

Inside, she kept smaller boxes filled with old tin cans and plastic spoons, a few torn paper plates, and some Styrofoam cups. A fire, fed with scraps of paper and sticks, burned constantly in a number-10 can that served as stove, furnace, and lantern. From it, Kai lit her cigarettes, the only luxury she allowed herself. She bought them with money she panhandled or earned by charging less entrepreneurial shopping bag ladies twenty-five cents a night for a space in her hut. She had no other income.

Kai's food was sometimes provided by the fruit and vegetable vendor on the corner or by the workers in the area who'd drop off a container of coffee and a sandwich or some donuts on their way to and from work. Many times, of course, she scrounged her meals from garbage cans. Well after midnight, she could be seen bent over the cans at Giordano's restaurant, one of the area's best, rummaging through its contents, sometimes devouring scraps on the spot but more often tossing them into a plastic shopping bag to eat later.

She rarely spoke, and when she did almost no one could

understand her. Her voice was a whisper, spoken as if to be heard only in her private world. You'd have to listen with your ear practically pressed to her mouth, and even then nothing would seem to make much sense. Patience would prove she was speaking English, but with a jumbled syntax like a code that protected her thoughts from intrusion.

Kai cannot tell her own story. Her hands are her biography. They are grotesque claws that testify to the frostbite that claimed her fingers, leaving ragged, blackened stumps. There are large scars, some as big around as a nickel, on her palms where infections set in. The remaining fingers are bent into talons.

During her years on the streets, her gums became infected, her teeth rotted to stumps; her bladder collapsed and she sat silently in her own urine. She stared into space, clawing at the lice in her hair, clinging tenaciously to her home.

For months, the nuns and volunteers would visit Kai in her hovel, bringing her food and caring for her. But Kai could not be coaxed to leave the harsh familiarity of her crate house for the uncertainty of the Dwelling Place, until one day a policeman who could no longer stand to see this fragment of humanity rot before his eyes began to tear apart Kai's shelter piece by piece. Terrified, Kai ran to the Dwelling Place and pummeled the door with her fists until someone let her inside. The Women's Shelter would have refused her: Name? Social Security number? Last address? Why did you leave there?

At the Dwelling Place, women were not asked *any* questions. They were not told to give up their money or to submit their bags for inventory. The Dwelling Place was, perhaps more than anything, a place of acceptance.

But it was not easy to be accepting. The ladies brought with them more baggage than was contained in their bags, and dealing with it proved exhausting.

Some were loud and violent, others painfully withdrawn. Some, like Kai, spoke their own private languages. Some were senile. One woman came with her feces packed in her shopping bags; one had to be prevented from drinking her urine.

Some were homeless because they were crazy, others were crazy because they were homeless. As one study by the Manhattan Bowery Corporation noted: "Lack of sleep alone can affect one's mental health. In order to survive on the streets, the women must maintain an almost constant alertness to danger. This inhibits sleep or any relaxation. Malnutrition, which can result in chemical imbalances to the blood, is another threat to mental health."

Some simply had mannerisms, eccentricities, that their families, their landlords, their doctors, their social workers could no longer tolerate but that fell short of what psychiatrists would have diagnosed as psychotic. Some were alcoholics who woke in the night writhing with the DTs. Others were addicted to drugs.

Many of the ladies were diseased. Tuberculosis and other lung disorders, the result of unrelieved exposure to the elements, are rampant among the homeless. So is anemia, caused by malnutrition and, sometimes, by the selling of blood for a few dollars a pint.

Almost all were infested with lice, and many bore the special stigmata of the shopping bag lady: leg ulcers. Before coming to the Dwelling Place, most of the women had slept sitting up on benches and in doorways. Former live-in volunteer Jonah Agassu, a onetime migrant worker who had lived for a time on the streets herself, explained the reluctance to lie down: "On the streets, a woman is more vulnerable to attack when she's prone. Men, well you know, men react differently to a woman when she's lying down. You understand? It does something to their heads, am I right? It's safer to sit up."

The constantly upright posture causes the valves in the veins of the legs to break down. The legs fill with fluid and begin to swell, sometimes reaching two or three times their normal size; the skin around the ankles becomes inflamed; the skin begins to bleed, and if the leg is not treated streaks of red—signs of infection—spread upward, until the lymph glands are contaminated and can no longer combat infection. If treated early, leg ulcers can be relatively harmless; ignored, they strip away the flesh and leave open, suppurating sores that smell like what they are—decaying meat.

For all their ideals, their cheerfulness, and their considerable strength, only a few months into their mission the nuns were overwhelmed. "We just couldn't handle all the ladies we had," Sister Nancy told me. "There were just too many of us. We were stepping all over each other and we were constantly at each others' throats. Things started getting violent."

Outbursts became increasingly frequent: one woman threw a vacuum cleaner through a window, another pulled a kitchen knife on one of the ladies. One woman attacked Sister Nancy, pinned her to the floor, and began beating her with her fists; it took three volunteers to drag her off. Sister Nancy, at least in the retelling, shrugged off the violence as an occupational hazard. "The ladies were 'off' a lot," she said, smiling. "They were acting out. Things were getting much too hostile. It was getting pretty tough to cope with."

The nuns were worn out. They begged their order to allow them to quit their nursing jobs, but their superiors, never overly supportive of the Dwelling Place "experiment," refused. The nuns' salaries were too important to the order. "We asked them to come to see the house, to see what we were doing, but they never came," Sister Nancy said.

"We were running on four hours' sleep a night, every night, and we were beginning to burn out. The house was becoming like a people-factory. Things were getting out of hand. We were emotionally wrecked. We agonized and we prayed and ultimately we decided that, while we could continue to feed everyone, we would be able to provide beds for only twelve ladies. The rest we would have to move along." It was spring 1978, and the Dwelling Place had been in operation for less than half a year.

At about the same time, the manager of the Times Square Motor Hotel approached the nuns. He had what he thought might be a mutually advantageous proposal. Caught in the pinch between crime and the porno trade, the hotel was suffering serious loss of business. He had already begun to take some public assistance trade—Phyllis was living in room 1226 and paying her $162-a-month rent from her SSI benefits—and he was looking for more. But he wanted to have more control over who his "guests" would be than he would have if he entered into a welfare contract with the city.

"I guess he saw us as a solution to the hotel's problems,"

Sister Nancy said. "He came to us and said if we would screen people for him, he would give them rooms at the welfare rate." The nuns were delighted. The hotel was not the luxury showplace it once had been. But it was no fleabag, either.

They stepped up efforts to get eligible ladies on welfare or SSI and move them into the hotel.

"We were not into asking for information," Jonah, the former live-in volunteer, recalled. "We were used to *listening* for information—getting it slowly without asking specific questions or filling out forms. When we found out something that we thought was important for the others to know, we'd share it with them. If we had tried pressure tactics some of the ladies would just have run out the door.

"We had to learn the ropes of the social services. Nobody helped us much. We were on our own. Sink or swim. We made a lot of mistakes, but in time we became rather expert. We convinced one welfare center to let us fill out the intake forms ourselves. That was half the battle. It saved everybody a lot of time and headaches."

It was not long before ladies began moving into the hotel. Among them was Kai.

After many weeks of listening to Kai's jumbled private language, one of the volunteers uncovered her last name. Deeper investigation revealed that Kai had once collected Social Security benefits and that she had accumulated nearly $3,000 in unclaimed payments.

She is receiving benefits regularly now and is still living at the hotel, watched over by a group made up mostly of former Dwelling Place volunteers who run low-cost activities for the ladies—bingo, dances, movies, things like that—and help them with their personal problems. "Kai is proof positive that even the most broken lives can be pieced back together," Sandy Bollada, one of the volunteers at the hotel, maintains.

Ironically, as ladies from the Dwelling Place were moving into the hotel, Phyllis was being forced out. Her rent had been increased by $15 a month at the same time her Social Security payments had been slashed by $25. She had little choice. On July 15, 1980, she gave up her room at the Times Square Motor Hotel.

She began to take her meals at the Dwelling Place, but she would not sleep there, nor in any shelter. Neither would she return to the hotel, even after the nuns told her they could help her get a room there at a rent she could afford. "She was adamant," Sister Nancy remembered. "To her that would have been too much like charity. She wouldn't even consider it. Her pride was involved, and Phyllis was a very proud woman."

And so Phyllis expended half a dollar for a locker at the Port Authority Bus Terminal to store all that she had saved of her belongings—four shopping bags of possessions—and took up residence on a waiting-room bench.

Dead
End

August 11, 1980. A driving rain hammered the pavement in front of 409 West 40th Street. Phyllis huddled at the entrance to the Dwelling Place and leaned on the buzzer. Sister Nancy rushed downstairs and flung open the door.

"Please," Phyllis pleaded. "Please let me stay. I've got nowhere else to go."

Sister Nancy pulled her drenched bags into the doorway and ushered Phyllis inside. Upstairs, the voice of John Chancellor filled the room with its measured resonance as he unraveled the intricacies of the Democratic national convention, under way half a mile away at Madison Square Garden.

It was not coincidence that Phyllis arrived at the Dwelling Place begging for sanctuary on the same day the convention opened. It was a matter of cause and effect.

Phyllis was one of hundreds of New Yorkers displaced by daily police rousts and roundups designed to get "undesirables" off midtown streets where 5,500 big-spending out-of-town delegates had come to nominate a candidate and have a good time.

The city spent more than $5 million on the convention—$400,000 just for a "welcoming kit" that included free tickets to theaters, Yankee games, and tourist spots—and officials expected the five-day extravaganza to generate at least $30 million in revenues. "We want to remind the rest of the country about the strengths of New York City—the richness, the diversity, the culture—to imprint that on the people's consciousness," said Robert Tierney, the mayor's chief of convention-related matters.

And so delegates saw a midtown Manhattan not often seen by New Yorkers themselves: scrubbed and freshly painted, free of litter and purged of much of its population. The Police Department laid on a force of 2,500 uniformed cops and 500 plainclothes officers just to patrol the streets surrounding the Garden, and the public morals division doubled its manpower in the neighborhood. As a reporter covering the convention, I watched cops prod scores of indigents into ceaseless migration or arrest them on charges of dubious legality.

"We're just trying to get them off the street," Inspector Emil Ciccotelli, chief of the morals division, told me at the time. "We don't want them hassling unsophisticated tourists and delegates who don't know what they're getting into."

By the time the convention opened, hundreds of arrests had been made, and the harassment of street people had become so intense that St. Francis of Assisi Church had opened its courtyard as a sanctuary. "What was going on was a nightmare," Father John Felice, pastor of the church, recalled. "So when we were approached with the idea of offering sanctuary, we didn't have to think about it much. We opened it up for the duration of the convention. Each night as many as 100 people stayed there, all huddled up with their bags and blankets. It was like a refugee camp."

The Port Authority Bus Terminal where Phyllis was living then was about half a mile from Madison Square Garden, but still within the Police Department's convention target area.

The terminal is a city in its own right, serving some 300,000 commuters and travelers daily with bars and bowling alleys, restaurants and luncheonettes, clothing stores, barbershops and beauty parlors, bookstores, newsstands, an Off-Track Betting parlor.

By day, the terminal serves as a funnel to midtown Manhattan, channeling workers to their jobs and tourists to the wonders of the Big Apple; by night it becomes a haven for dope dealers and junkies, runaway teenagers, pimps, hookers, and homosexual hustlers, pickpockets, confidence men, and panhandlers, winos and drifters, and people like Phyllis with no place else to go.

The banks of railway lockers along the walls of the station's concourses provided Phyllis with the closest thing she had to a home: a tan metal box designed to hold two suitcases, or, as it happened, four shopping bags laden with all her possessions. The cost was fifty cents for twenty-four hours—or every time the locker was opened. Phyllis would have to make sure she did not go into her locker more than once a day. And if she let twenty-four hours go by without paying her half dollar, someone from the storage company would come around to empty the locker into a trash bag.

She would have to pay to reclaim her belongings, which meant, perhaps, that she would have to abandon them. Still, the locker beat the alternative, which was to have no place at all to put her things.

Phyllis slept on benches in the waiting room, moving frequently to avoid the police and the gangs of youths who prowled the station preying on the defenseless. At night, the terminal was a deadly place.

Officially, police designated it as part of patrol sector Adam, but street cops called it by another name: "The Sewer." In 1980, fully 15 percent of the felony crime committed in the Midtown South precinct, one of the city's toughest, took place there. The Eighth Avenue subway station on the lower levels of the terminal boasted the highest felony crime rate of any in the city.

But in that one week of August 1980, crime took a holiday. Phyllis Iannotta was not there to enjoy it. Port Authority cops had chased her out of the terminal, and city cops had pushed her off the streets. She not only had no home to go to, she had *nowhere* to go: nowhere to sleep, nowhere even to sit for an hour to rest. Everywhere she went the cops would move her on. Finally, she wound up at the Dwelling Place, as Sister Nancy puts it, "frustrated, angry, agitated, and confused."

"We knew she could be very difficult sometimes," Sister Nancy said. "She was always ready for a fight and she had a mouth on her that would make a truck driver blush. But she was a good person and there was never any question about her staying. We're here for the Phyllises of the world."

And so it was that Phyllis came to occupy the armchair by the fireplace near the television set in the large living room on the second floor. "She liked it there," Sister Nancy said.

"That was her place. She kept her bags next to the chair, and if she caught anyone sitting in it it was grounds for a fight; she was very possessive of that old chair by the fireplace. Phyllis could get pretty nasty, so if one of the ladies was sitting there, she'd usually move when Phyllis entered the room."

At the Dwelling Place, Phyllis is remembered as a kind of schizoid paradox who could be friendly and helpful one minute and hostile—even violent—the next. Her conversation would jump from smiling pleasantries to biting sarcasm without apparent provocation.

Gloria, the gossipy, unofficial housemother, had seen scores of ladies come and go at the Dwelling Place. "Phyllis," she said, "was a real yeller. Boy oh boy could she yell. You'd never know what would set her off. Sometimes she'd just start for no reason at all. You know, she'd start mumbling under her breath, then all of a sudden, pow! She'd start screaming her head off. You'd never know why, that was the strange thing. 'Cause other times, she could be sweet as pie. She'd laugh and joke and she'd share cigarettes and things like that. Oh yeah. And she was real fair. She'd take anybody's side who was being picked on. She'd stand up for the underdog."

"Oh, she'd speak her mind all right," Bob Johnston, the volunteer overnight man, told me. "She didn't care who was listening. She liked to provoke people, to get them stirred up, to test them. I remember once she kept praising Hitler and making pro-Nazi comments within earshot of one of the Jewish ladies. Do I think she *was* pro-Nazi? Not her. Not for a minute. She was just looking for a reaction. She liked to create a scene where she would be the center of attraction. She had a kind of cussedness about her.

"She could be very mean. She'd sit down at dinner with

maybe thirty other women in the room—she had on these thick glasses and a sharp nose that made her look like a hawk—and she'd look down her nose and make these snide comments.

"On the other side of the coin, she had a great laugh, an inviting laugh. She invited others to laugh with her. But, you know, the ladies can sit next to each other night after night and watch television or even dance with each other once in a while at parties, but a lot of them don't really relate to each other very well. They have their own concerns; they're in their own world."

When Phyllis laughed, former volunteer Ann Quintano reflected, "it seemed almost like a lie, as if she were flirting with letting down her armor. But she couldn't let down her defenses. She had been hurt too many times. For her, there was safety in the distance she put between herself and others."

"Five Sugars" Grace remembered Phyllis as "a real Eyetalian. When she was in a good mood you'd hear her singing 'O Sole Mio,' stuff like that. When she was in a bad mood, she'd curse the devil out of you in two languages! She was a tough old bird. Full of fight. Did I like her? Can't say as I did, can't say as I didn't. She was a kinda funny gal. Moody."

Phyllis frightened Nickel Louise. "I don't know about that woman. I just don't know. She was angry and she carried a stick. Did anybody tell you that, Little Papa? Well, sir, yes she did. A stick with a point on the end, And you know what? She would shake it at you like she was gonna hit you. Yes she would. Why, you never knew what she'd do. No sir. You'd never know. It's people like her who get called bag ladies."

To Margaret, a middle-aged widow who used to work

as a waitress at Schrafft's, Phyllis was "as unpredictable as the weather. She could be bright and she could be cloudy, if you know what I mean. I used to steer clear of her because *I* know enough to come in from the rain, if you know what I mean."

Phyllis quickly settled into a rhythm at the Dwelling Place. "She was always the first up in the morning," Jonah recalled. "She'd be right there at 6:30 helping me wake the others. I can still hear her calling 'Rise and shine! Rise and shine!' She could be a very pleasant lady in the morning."

By nine, after a hefty breakfast of hot cereal, toast, juice, and coffee, Phyllis helped with the dishes. And maybe after that, Jonah said, she'd "pitch in and help me in the kitchen chopping vegetables for the soup. Sometimes she'd ask me to help her pick out clothes from the clothing room downstairs. She didn't want much and she wasn't fussy. She liked dark colors and blues. It was hard to find sizes that fit, though. She was so short and she was rather stout. All misproportioned."

At 10:00 A.M., the house would close until dinner time at five "to keep the ladies from hanging around all day and vegetating," as senior nun, Sister Naureen Kelly, put it. Then Phyllis would take a shopping bag, heave herself out of her armchair, and go out "on the stroll."

"Phyllis was a loner most of the time, but sometimes she'd go out with Bernice," Sister Nancy said. "Bernice was just about her only close friend here. Everybody was a little afraid of Bernice. Like Phyllis, she had a real mouth on her. She was rather—how would you put it?—intimidating. But for a time those two were inseparable. They'd sit together talking a blue streak. Sometimes neither one of them would be making an ounce of sense. It was as if they were holding separate conversations, talking about completely different things. But they would laugh and nod as if they were sharing jokes. I couldn't make out what they were talking about. But they were on the same wavelength."

They made an incongruous pair: Phyllis, five feet two, squat and hunched over, dressed in dark colors, with those bottle-thick glasses perched on her beak of a nose, and Bernice, six feet two, 180 pounds, black as ebony and ramrod straight, dressed always in bold-colored caftans and a curly green fright wig under an elaborate turban that made her look like a sci-fi Amazon princess.

Bernice lives at the Times Square Motor Hotel now and is taking medication for her schizophrenia. She has exchanged her green wig for a more mundane auburn flip and has abandoned her turbans. Now she prides herself on finding bargains in Times Square thrift shops.

"Back when I was staying at the Dwelling I was very mentally ill," she told me with disarming frankness. "Phyllis was pretty sick too, I guess you could say. But she was my friend. Oh yes, we sure did kick up some sand! We used to joke a lot about everything. She had a funny laugh. It'd make you laugh too just to hear it. I miss Phyllis. She was good company."

Together the two of them would leave the relative calm of the Dwelling Place and venture through Hell's Kitchen, slowly making their way to Holy Cross Church through the underbelly of Times Square.

"First, we'd walk over to the Port," Bernice recalls. "Phyllis used to like it there. In summer it's air-conditioned. Real nice. We'd sit there a spell, then maybe we'd go down to the pier and watch the ships. We'd get some lunch at

Holy Cross and Phyllis would go inside and say her prayers and things, then she'd buy us coffee and we'd sit on the steps—that was one of Phyllis's favorite spots, her hangout you could say—and we'd smoke and talk about old movie stars, Cary Grant, Betty Grable, all the great old ones or maybe bandleaders and singers. She liked the Dorsey brothers and I liked the Ink Spots.

"That's how we'd spend the day, talking about old times. You see, our old times were a lot better than our new times. Me, I was a sewing-machine operator until I got mental problems and lost my job, and Phyllis, she worked all her life. She told me she worked at the Brooklyn Navy Yard. A real good job. We weren't always shopping bag ladies."

Bernice paused and puffed meditatively on a Kool. She looked past me, deep in thought. "It's awful out there," she said, speaking as if to herself. "The junkies they keep stepping up in front of you and hassling you and the hookers they call you names 'cause they think you worse than them. And the kids, them tough kids, they always be grabbin' at your bags and you gotta scream at them real good so's they go away. Phyllis, she took to carrying a stick, a stick with a point, and she wasn't afraid to use it."

She smiled in recollection. "Phyllis, she was like me. Real tough. But, you know, you got to be tough out on the street. Got to be when you're living out there. That's why the Dwelling was so good. You'd get to come inside. Get some rest, get some food, and those nuns, why, they're just so considerate and thoughtful. You can *confide* in them. Those Dwelling people they'd remind you you were a human being. Why, the only person you knowed before like that was your mother. Yessir, just like your mama."

"One of the big problems with Phyllis was that she liked it here too much," Sister Nancy told me one night. "She wasn't moving. She was able to take care of herself and she was getting two checks. We'd made deals with some of the hotels for special rates. Now Phyllis could afford a room.

"I understood how she felt about the Times Square, her bad feelings about being forced to leave. But it wasn't just that hotel, it was *any* hotel. We found other places she could afford—the Woodstock, for example. A lot of elderly people stay there. Phyllis could have afforded it. She said she'd go, too. But then when we talked about it she'd say she had to have a room with a kitchenette, which of course was not possible. There were no such rooms. Or she'd make an appointment to see a room and never go. It became pretty clear that Phyllis would not leave without a push."

Sister Nancy closed her eyes and shook her head from side to side. "That was how 'rotation' got started," she said sadly. "All twelve beds were filled and we were beginning to run out of chairs. This seemed like a way to take care of two problems. It would give ladies who weren't trying to find a place an inducement to start looking and it would free up beds for others. We weren't crazy about it, but at least it would give everyone a chance to spend *some* time inside."

After four days of living inside, the ladies were expected to rotate out for three days so other women could take their places. They were given "contracts"—slips of paper indicating which days they were allowed to stay—and, although sometimes the nuns would look the other way when a volunteer sneaked one of the ladies back into the house, the rule was usually enforced, rain or shine.

There were many complaints about the new rule, from both residents and volunteers. But Sister Naureen, the tough-minded house administrator who had spent most of her life working in institutions, remained firm. "It may not have been ideal," she told me, "but it was consistent, something the ladies could count on. How does one care for the mentally ill—and most of our ladies here are mentally ill in one way or another—how does one do that? I say with consistency."

"Phyllis had been put out of the house occasionally even before the whole rotation thing," according to Ann Quintano. "Sometimes she would be aggressive and someone would have to tell her to leave and not come back until the next day, or even for a couple of days." Yet that happened only rarely, and Phyllis seemed able to cope with it. Rotation, however, was a rule, and Phyllis did not react well to any regulation.

"She would sit across the street on the steps to the church and glare up at the window all night," volunteer Sandy Bollada remembered. "It was like an accusation."

Phyllis began to deteriorate. "She became much more disoriented," Sandy said. "She would still come for dinner, but after dinner when she was supposed to leave she'd yell that it was not her night out. The nuns would show her the contract chart and she'd call them liars. She felt they were plotting against her."

Phyllis became increasingly troublesome.

Entries in the Dwelling Place daily log tell the story. "Phyllis poured a jar of peanuts into a sink. Big flood. Said she was trying to clean the sink." "Phyllis poured shampoo into the toilet." "Phyllis angry and raving, had to tell her to leave. Can't come back till breakfast." "Phyllis very off. She punched Monica Lanza."

228

Ann Quintano remembered one particular incident:

"It was late and the ladies who were supposed to be on rotation were leaving. Everyone, that is, except Phyllis. She just sat at the dining room table with a Styrofoam cup of coffee, taking her time. She seemed to have no notion of leaving at all, even after several requests. When she finished her coffee, she got up and got another cup. She ignored us, acted as if we weren't there.

"This was a battle of wills. I can't say as I blamed her. She felt that this was her home, and who was I to put her out? I was so exasperated.

"She refused to be controlled, to be taken for granted, to be made to bend to *our* rules in *her* place. And me, I'm sorry to say, I was on a real authority trip, unable to deal with her on her own terms.

"We finally wound up downstairs, God only knows how, and that's when the yelling and screaming started. I was stuck at the door with her because I couldn't bring myself to slam the door in her face. That's when she started grabbing for my glasses. She of all people knew how incapacitating that could be.

"When she couldn't get hold of my glasses she grabbed a cluster of my hair and held on. I mean she *really* held on." Ann winced at the memory. "I couldn't get free without tearing hair from my head. We were bellowing at each other and making such a racket that Sister Nancy came running down from the fourth floor. She brought things back under control. But Phyllis left there with a fistful of my hair."

A few weeks later, Phyllis attacked Sister Nancy, grabbed her by the neck, and raked her throat with her fingernails. "I tried to tell her she needed medication," Sister Nancy said, "but she refused to see a doctor. 'You're the sick one,' she'd say. Her voice was like acid. The only thing I knew that would calm her down before she really went off was the past. The past was Phyllis's medicine.

"She used to like to talk to me about the old Italian ways, about making tomato sauce—we Neapolitans call it gravy—from scratch. She'd tell me recipes her mother taught her and we'd talk about the pushcarts and the Italian groceries with everything hanging from the ceiling. She would talk about Santa Lucia and she knew all the old superstitions. She was a great believer in the *malocc'*, the evil eye. She knew about all that from her childhood in Brooklyn; I remembered them from growing up in the Italian part of the Village around Thompson Street. And so when she was having a bad time, we'd talk about the past. The past was what pacified her."

But when Phyllis returned to the streets her present canceled out the calming memories of the past. She stopped bathing and her body crawled with lice. She smelled. Her feet began to swell and sores formed on them. She seemed not to notice. She grew more and more delusional. "When she came for dinner," Sister Naureen remembered, "she would talk about her conversations with the president. She stopped making any sense."

"This is how sad it was," Sister Nancy began, and then she told me a detail that arrested me like no other: "I remember her laboring over a crossword puzzle all day—she loved crossword puzzles—and when she finished it she showed it to me. The blanks were just filled in with gibberish."

One day Phyllis appeared at the door of the Dwelling Place with blood streaming from her mouth. Her head was gashed and she had a bruise the size of a silver dollar on her cheek.

"She was crying," Sister Nancy remembered. "She said

that she was sitting on a crate by the vegetable stand up at the corner when a man came up to her and offered her five dollars. I don't know what he said to her but she refused to take his money. He apparently insisted. She must have said something to him. Maybe she cursed him out. Maybe she didn't say anything. I don't know. Anyway, she said he hit her with a stick and punched her face. It wasn't the first time one of our ladies had been beaten up. It was happening a lot that summer. There are a lot of crazies in this neighborhood. Anyway, I wanted Phyllis to go to the emergency room and get stitches but she wouldn't have anything to do with hospitals."

That was March 27, 1981. Four days later, a log entry shows that Phyllis was "healing well" after the attack. But her mental deterioration accelerated.

The journal entries tell the story:

April 1: "Phyllis a bit off starting about 11:30 P.M. and through much of the night. Yelling. Finally fell asleep."

April 4: "Phyllis angry. Foul-mouthed the ladies. Asked her to be quiet and she started raving. She stormed out. Didn't come back for supper."

April 6: "Phyllis disruptive. She kept opening and slamming the window. She was told to leave at 2:30 A.M. Very angry."

April 11: "Phyllis very tired."

April 13: "Phyllis tired, but off."

April 15: "Phyllis very off."

April 19: "Phyllis very off. Disruptive. Yelling, cursing."

Five days later, April 24, 1981, was a Friday, and Phyllis's night out on rotation. A light rain fell.

Sister Naureen recited the events of that night as if she had repeated them many times, as I supposed she had—to the police and to herself. "Phyllis was pleasant that night when she left," she said. "Nancy was supposed to be working, but she was sick and I took her shift. Anyway, I was in the process of asking people to leave, sort of shooing them along, when I came to Phyllis in the dining room. I expected a fight. But she simply got up, picked up her bag, and left. She and Monica Lanza left together. They used to go at each other all the time. But when they weren't trying to kill each other they were good friends." They left about 8:15.

Four hours later, Monica pounded frantically at the door. Jonah, who had come on duty about midnight, rushed downstairs and flung open the door. "Monica was very agitated," she remembered. "She had a gash on her hand, a bad cut. It needed stitches but she wouldn't let anyone touch it. She had poured some kind of powder, like baby powder or something, into the cut. When I asked her what happened she was very vague. She wasn't making much sense. I asked her 'Where's Phyllis?' and she just said 'I don't know.' I tried to get more out of her, but she just clammed up. Finally I made her a cup of tea and put her to bed."

The next morning, Sister Nancy bathed Monica's hand but she still refused treatment. "She was out of the house by five," the nun recalled. "I guess you could say we knew things weren't exactly kosher, but we had no inkling of what had really happened."

Then, about 5:15 A.M., Jonah went outside to get some air. "Just outside the front door I found a pocketbook," Jonah told me. "It was Phyllis's. I recognized it because I had helped her pick it out in the clothing room. That's when I began to worry."

At 7:45 Officer Charles Desfosse knocked on the Dwelling Place door.

"He asked if I'd look at a body in the parking lot out back to see if I could identify it," Sister Naureen said. Desfosse led her to the spot beside the dumpster and lifted the dirty brown blanket that covered the body. "Phyllis," the nun told him. "Phyllis Iannotta."

Who
Killed
Phyllis
Iannotta?

Sister Nancy broke the news to the ladies of the Dwelling
Place. "I called them together and we sat right here in the
front room and talked about it," she told me one Friday
night. "We were all pretty shaken, stunned I guess you
could say. Who wouldn't be? There were some tears, some
crying, you know, but not as much as you might think. Many
of these women have seen so much they, well, they just
can't show the depth of their emotion anymore.

"There was a sense of calm, at first. The ladies talked
about Phyllis, you know, like in a tribute. One woman, I
think it was Dorothy, remembered how Phyllis loved to
dance at parties. Grace talked about how if ever anybody
needed something, a cigarette or something, Phyllis would
share. Bernice talked about her laugh. Bernice took it hard.
They were good friends. It was tough on her.

"It was all so sad. The whole thing, so senseless, so awful that she had to go out on the street and get killed. We were all hurt and angry. I, for one, was incredibly angry at whoever it was who killed Phyllis—at the senseless brutality of it all—and even angrier, I think, at the entire system that put women on the streets. Oh yes, and I think it is safe to say that we were all afraid. That man was still out there."

Weeks had given way to months and months to years as I slowly assembled a portrait of Phyllis Iannotta from fragments of memory and pieces of paper, and her murder—a killing without clues, motive, or a known witness—remained unsolved. Police in that time learned little more than they had when Dominick Nisi's grim discovery brought them to the parking lot behind the Dwelling Place.

They had come in swarms—uniformed cops, city detectives, and Port Authority police, all of them seeking scraps of information that when pieced together might make some sense of the senseless savagery. They had trooped in and out of the Dwelling Place all that day, questioning the nuns, the volunteers, the ladies.

"I'll never forget it," Ann Quintano told me afterward. "It was terrible. The cops just kept asking questions, questions, questions. And all the while, Phyllis's body lay out there in the parking lot."

The body was not removed until well into the afternoon. When I asked Detective Longo about it on the day of the murder, he looked at me with bored impatience. "Look," he said, "I don't mean to be vulgar, but she's not going anywhere." It was his way of telling me he was tired of my questions.

"I'll never forget one particular scene," Quintano continued. "The man from the morgue came into the kitchen to wash his hands. He turned on the water and got it just the right temperature. Then he put his hands under the water and he rubbed them together, all real matter-of-fact, you know, nothing special, just washing his hands. And I remember watching Phyllis's blood run down the drain."

All that day, detectives had canvassed the neighborhood door to door. Police officers had taken down the license-plate numbers of every car parked in and around the Port Authority lot. Their owners were tracked down and questioned. Cops knocked on every door on the block, they questioned the early-morning sanitation workers, the night man at Daytop Village across the street, the workers at the all-night fruit and vegetable stand on the corner, the prostitutes: "Did you see anything? Did you hear anything? Where were you last night between the hours of 8:00 P.M. and two in the morning?" Questions and more questions.

I phoned Longo daily in the first weeks after the murder with my own questions. They were always the same. Any suspects? Any leads? Our conversations were brief. My calls irritated him. He was making no headway. He kept me at arm's length, refusing to discuss details of the case with me. "It's under investigation," he'd tell me and the conversation would end.

Finally, two months after the murder, I caught Longo in his office in the tenth precinct's second-floor squad room. Maybe he had come to admire my persistence. Maybe he was just wearing down.

"This case worries me," he admitted. "It looked for a while like there might be a nut out there looking to take out shopping bag ladies." A few days after Phyllis's murder, he said, another homeless woman had been found slain a few blocks away. "The M.O. was completely different," Longo said. "I don't think they're related, but you never know. You can't be too sure."

The Iannotta case became his top priority. "We went back out there every day from ten in the morning until way after midnight for days. We even stopped cars going past the scene early in the morning on the long shot that one of them might be a regular commuter on that street who could have gone by on the night of the murder and seen something. People must have thought we were crazy. But we wanted to get this guy. We wanted him bad."

Longo waved a white lined note pad in my face. "Look at this," he said, slapping it on his cluttered metal desk. Four full pages were covered with names. "We've questioned every one of these people. Every damn one of them. It's not that we're not trying. We got leads. But none of them are materializing."

Among the names on the list was a Port Authority cop named Frank Sabatino.

Sabatino told detectives that he had seen a man in the parking lot at about 11:30 that night: "He was black, about six-one and maybe about 180 pounds. He had on a dark jacket and dark pants with black sneakers and he was sitting on top of an old car seat someone had thrown in the middle of the lot. I chased him out."

When Sabatino returned to the lot about 2:00 or 2:30 A.M., the man was there again, standing in front of the dumpster in the rear of the lot. "He was acting crazy," Sabatino told detectives, "waving his arms and talking to himself."

Sabatino ordered the man to leave. "He was moving out when I got a radio call to another job. I never did see whether he actually left the lot."

Had Sabatino seen the killer? Had Helen Kehayas? Nobody may ever know.

Longo believes they saw two different people. "The descriptions don't really match up. Naturally, we looked for people meeting both descriptions but that was pretty much an exercise in futility." He snorted. "You got any idea how many black guys in sneakers there are in that neighborhood?"

Philip Gennaro took the news of his sister's murder with a mixture of horror and disbelief. Detectives found him at Kilroy's bar and broke the news to him in a few short, unemotional sentences. As Phyllis's only living relative, they said, he would have to identify the body. The next afternoon he showed up at the morgue with Joe Quagliano, his friend from the One-Forty Bookstore. "Popeye took the news real bad," Quagliano remembered. "He was drunk that day and I brought along a couple of containers of black coffee to sober him up in the taxi. He kept saying over and over 'It can't be my sister. They gotta have the wrong person.'

"It was a terrible thing to experience," Quagliano said. "They wheeled her out and the body was almost completely covered with a shroud. She looked like a nun with just part of her face showing, about a six-inch circle. She was completely discolored and disfigured.

"I knew it was her because she used to come into the store sometimes. But Popeye kept insisting it was not his sister." Quagliano imitated Philip's drunken Brooklynese. " 'It's somebody else. It ain't my Fay.' That's what he always called her, Fay. He kept it up for maybe ten minutes, until finally I said, 'Popeye, let's go outside for a few minutes and get some air.' We went into an adjoining room and I said, 'Popeye just tell me. Is it your sister?' He broke down. 'That's my sister,' he said. And I said, 'Sign the paper that it's your sister and you can go get a drink.' So when I said that, he went back and made the identification. Then I took him back to 42nd Street, gave him a few bucks, and he went out and got his bottle."

Three days later, Philip stood unsteadily over an open grave at St. Raymond's Cemetery in the Bronx. It was an indigent's grave, supplied gratis by the cemetery at the request of the Dwelling Place. Three other adults and a child had been buried previously in that same grave, in the shade of a gnarled oak tree in a corner surrounded by modest granite tombstones.

Neighboring stones revealed that at Phyllis's head were the remains of John Haggerty, deceased the last day of January 1920; her feet pointed toward the final resting place of Francesco DelVecchio, dead since December 4, 1915. No stone would mark her grave.

Father Robert Rappleyea, who had comforted Phyllis in life, intoned the burial rites of the Roman Catholic Church over her body. "Comfort us in our sorrow at the death of our sister. Let our faith be our consolation and eternal life our hope. . . ." When all had been said, the priest picked up a handful of soil and threw it lightly onto the plain pine box, committing the body of Phyllis Iannotta to the "earth from which it was made."

Also standing over the grave were the nuns of the Dwelling Place, several volunteers, about half a dozen homeless women, and Richard Hansen, his wife and children, who had learned of Phyllis's death in the *Daily News*.

Conspicuously absent was Monica Lanza.

Lanza had disappeared several days after the murder, and I had tried in vain to track her down—in shelters, on soup lines, in the Port Authority Bus Terminal. More than a year had passed and I had given up hope of ever finding her when a feature story appeared about the Traveler's Hotel, a former Times Square whorehouse that the Westside Cluster—the nonprofit group that runs the drop-in center for homeless women on West 30th Street—had just converted into a residence for homeless women. The residents, the story indicated, were all veterans of the streets. "But today," the article went on, "all these women have their own rooms, where they can come in from the physical and psychological cold, get a cup of coffee, relax around a television set—and most of all, get a good night's sleep."

The article quoted several of the thirty-five women who had moved into the hotel. One of them was Monica Lanza.

I talked to the reporter who wrote the story. "Monica's a very nice lady," she said. "A little crazy, maybe, but nice. You shouldn't have any trouble getting her to talk to you."

The Traveler's looked as I had expected it to: outside, a shabby side-street hotel with a broken neon sign; inside, steep stairs and narrow corridors leading to nondescript rooms. Monica Lanza was a surprise. She looked nothing as I had remembered her from my momentary view when she was hauled yelling and struggling into the tenth precinct station house the morning after the murder.

She answered my knock with a friendly smile. I introduced myself and told her why I had come, but she didn't seem to be listening. She seemed glad to see me. It was clear she did not have many visitors and she was lonely. She welcomed me inside with a grandiose sweep of the arm. She was in her sixties, short and frail with neatly trimmed

240

gray hair and glasses. She wore a pretty pastel pink suit.

The room was small and illuminated by a single bare bulb in the center of a high ceiling. A twin bed, covered with a gold spread, was against one wall. An upturned cardboard box covered with a clean white towel served as a nightstand. A simple chest of drawers stood next to the window. Everything was scrubbed and orderly. Monica, whose SSI payments were paying her rent, had moved in shortly after the Cluster opened the hotel. She offered me the only chair in the room, and took a seat on the bed.

"Do you like my room?" she asked. Before I could answer she offered, "*I* love it. After what I've been through . . ." She paused and looked directly at me. "Well, it's just so nice to feel human again."

Bella English was right. Monica was anything but reticent.

"I was what they called a shopping bag lady," she began. "For four years I got my meals from garbage cans. Yes, young man, garbage cans. And I would lay my head wherever I could. I had no roof over my head, you see. No. Doorways were my home and cardboard boxes . . ." Her voice trailed off and she fumbled with her hands in her lap.

"It wasn't always like that, of course," she began again. "I used to be an infant nurse. All the best families. I took care of their little ones." She rattled off a list of names and addresses on the posh Upper East Side. She spoke of summers in Southampton and winters in the south of France. As she spoke, she began to affect a grand British accent. "I traveled in the best circles in those days. All very wealthy people, society people." They were people, she said, who entertained the likes of Herbert Hoover and the duchess of Windsor, Ray Bolger and Fred Astaire.

"But, you know, in my profession you never stay with

a family for long. By the time a baby was three I'd move on. I never had any problem finding work, of course. I had all the best references."

Unasked, Monica was giving me her life story.

"When my daughter was only fourteen months old, my husband got mugged. He came home all bloody. He was badly beaten. Well, he suffered some brain damage and he lost his job. I had a baby and I couldn't work. We were in trouble. He started drinking and he'd come home drunk and hit me. I was trying to take care of him and take care of the baby and everything. Well, to make a long story short, I wound up in the hospital. The police had to take me. They took my daughter away from me. I had to give my little girl to the policeman but I didn't think it was her, it was John-John Kennedy. I gave the policeman John-John Kennedy . . ."

Monica dropped the British accent and spoke in a small and childlike voice. "When I got out I went on welfare. I found it all very degrading, all the questions, the prying into your life. I suppose they have to ask some of those things, but sometimes I think they just like to pry."

Then one October day in 1977, she said, "I had a fight with my caseworker. She yelled at me. Yelled at *me*. The nerve! Well that was the last straw. I tore up the papers and threw them at her and left. And I went to live in the streets."

Monica pulled an embroidered hanky from her sleeve and dabbed at her eyes.

"I had no place to go after that, and I went to Penn Station to sleep on the benches there. That's how I found out that there were women who actually lived in the bathroom, who slept on the floor there. On the *floor!* I tell you

242

I was shocked." She laughed—a short, high-pitched whine. "Pretty soon I was right there with them."

Then one day, she told me, she was washing herself in the ladies' room sink when the police burst in. "They forced us all to leave. I was soaking wet and they wouldn't even let me dry off. They made me go outside like that. Oh, it was awful. And what could I do? Who could I turn to? Nobody listens to you when you're a bag lady, young man. Nobody."

Monica moved crosstown to Grand Central Terminal. She wasn't there long before she was mugged and the contents of her shopping bags were stolen. "I was hurt very badly, but I had nowhere to go. I just had to suffer alone. That's when I decided I would have to learn the art of unreality. That's when I decided to go to Cambodia." She squinted at me, gauging my reaction.

"Cambodia?"

"Well," she explained, "I'd see all these pictures of little Cambodian orphans living on nothing but mud and rocks. You know, I was raised in an orphanage until a German family took me in back in the thirties. Well, I said, if those little Cambodian orphans can do it, I can do it. So I went to Cambodia.

"One night I found a large cardboard refrigerator box and some plastic bags and I built a little Cambodian hut. I had a little cardboard box and a tin can I used for a potty and I brought in the things I needed off the streets."

Monica's voice was measured and calm as she told me of her life without a home. She could have been telling me about a trip to the store.

"You'd be amazed at the things you can find on the streets," she continued. "I would get my food from garbage cans, even my clothes. Around restaurants, don't you know, you can always find good things to eat. They always prepare too much and that's the food you take. Not plate scrapings or anything. One thing, though. Never eat donuts from the garbage. No. Not donuts. I saw a man urinate on a bag of them once. No. You can eat anything but donuts."

Once, she said, "I found Jackie Kennedy's black mouton coat in a trash can." She smiled a secret smile. "I called it that, you see. The art of unreality. All part of the art of unreality. Sometimes I would walk all the way up to the marina at 79th Street and go sit beside the boats and pretend I was rich."

She pulled a box from under her bed, opened it, and retrieved several small, painstakingly crocheted dolls. "I made these myself for Amy Carter," she said, placing each doll carefully on the bed and smoothing it out. "This is Nancy Reagan," she said gently lifting one of the dolls. "And that is Princess Di. That one is Jackie Kennedy and that one . . ."

Each of the dolls was named for a celebrity. Monica caressed them fondly and spoke to each of them in baby talk. She was drifting off into her own private world, far from me, far from her Cambodia.

I interrupted. "Monica, do you remember Phyllis Iannotta? You lived together at the Dwelling Place."

Monica hastily gathered up her dolls and put them back in their box as if to prevent them from hearing what was about to be said. She sat rigidly upright on the bed and her eyes darted suspiciously around the room.

"You want to know about the murder, don't you?" she asked. I nodded. "Please tell me what happened that night."

She shook her head rapidly from side to side. "I don't

know what happened," she whined. "I told the police. I don't know. Nobody believes me. I . . . don't . . . know."

"Well," I tried, "what do you remember about that night?"

"All right," Monica said, her voice small and petulant. "I'll tell you. You write this down." Then she began to recite as if she had told the story many times before. "We were sitting on the stoop a few doors down from the Dwelling Place waiting for Jonah. She came on duty at midnight and we thought she would let us in. Sometimes she'd let people in on their nights out so they wouldn't have to be outside.

"We were there a long time and I said to Phyllis, 'Phyllis, I'm going to sleep' and I leaned my head against the door and fell asleep. Phyllis said she was going to stay awake and smoke. She was on the steps below me.

"Well, at one point I woke up. I don't know what time it was or anything. I started to walk down the steps and I didn't even turn to look to see where Phyllis was when I got hit from behind. I threw my arm up to defend myself and I got hit. I just ran and ran and ran. I ran to the Port and I saw a girl there I knew and I said, 'Have you seen Phyllis?' See, I didn't know what happened to Phyllis. I just didn't know.

"I bought a box of Ammons powder and put it on the cut to coagulate the blood. Then I went to the Dwelling Place and they let me in.

"The next day," she continued, "I was sitting over on Ninth Avenue when the cops came and grabbed me like a common criminal. A common criminal. They dragged me over to their car and they pushed me in." Her words came faster, louder, as she recalled the incident. "I kept telling them I didn't know a goddamned thing. I didn't know anything. I didn't see anything. I was crying. I said, 'It's not my fault I'm alive.' It *wasn't* my fault. They took me into that awful parking lot. Oh, my God, they made me go back there. I told them I didn't know anything. I didn't see anything. Please don't make me go back there . . ."

Her voice filled with urgency and fear. She began to whimper. "I hid out after that," she said. "I was afraid that man might come back. Do you think he would do that? What do you think?"

Cops continued to bring in suspects for months after the murder. In May, they questioned a messenger with a record of arrests for purse snatching and credit-card fraud who fit Kehayas's description. "We couldn't place the guy at the scene," Longo said. "He wasn't our boy."

In June, detectives interrogated a teenager from Covenant House after his buddy told police he had bragged about committing the murder. "He was a bad actor and possibly capable of that kind of violence," the detective maintained. "But he was at Covenant House all that night and could prove it."

And in July, police were ready to charge a convicted sex offender who had been arrested as he tried to force a bag lady into his car in front of the Port Authority Bus Terminal. "We thought he was our guy," Longo said. "But the sonofabitch had an airtight alibi. He was in jail when the murder took place.

"It looked like our only hope," Longo conceded, "was that we'd catch the murderer for some other crime and he'd get careless and we'd link him somehow to the Iannotta case."

Longo retired from the force in 1983. The killer was still at large.

Years have passed since I stood over the broken body of Phyllis Iannotta in that parking lot in Hell's Kitchen, since I began sifting the shards of her life for a story that could not be told in 600 words on deadline. The grass has grown thick over her grave; there is no trace of where she was buried. When I visited it with my eight-year-old daughter, who was five when Phyllis was murdered, she asked me who killed Phyllis.

I told her I didn't know.